EXIT STRATEGY
Leaving this Life with Grace and Gratitude

by
Kelsey Collins

ChaseHawk Publishing
P.O. Box 303
Sisters, Oregon 97759
www.ExitStrategy-thebook.com

With all blessings

EXIT STRATEGY
Leaving this Life with Grace and Gratitude

by
Kelsey Collins

Exit Strategy... may be purchased from local and online booksellers or directly from the publisher:

ChaseHawk Publishing
PO Box 303
Sisters, Oregon 97759
www.ExitStrategy-thebook.com

ChaseHawk Publishing
ISBN 0-9818621-0-1

Endorsements for EXIT STRATEGY

"This book is a loving tribute to Bee Landis, showing her spunk, humor and wisdom. Bee was a blessing to everyone who met her. We all remember her with love."

Louise Hay, author of You Can Heal Your Life.

"On rare occasion, someone writes a book that actually shakes up the status quo in an area. Kelsey Collins has deftly and courageously done just that in *Exit Strategy*. She takes on the very essence of elder care in western society and forces our guilt, shame and fear out into the open. Even more importantly, she explodes the myth that these or any negative emotions must predominate the process of aging and dying. She elucidates brilliantly how mirth and lightness of being can guide the exit process and underscores repeatedly the learning that can occur at the moment of departure, for both the patient and the caregiver. Her writing provides deeply moving testament to the depth of healing that occurs when one faces one's own fears and charts a course to forgiveness. Furthermore, it humanizes the aging process in a 'no-holds-barred' manner that gently forces us to recognize we are not only all in this together; we are also all going to exit at some point, and maybe, just maybe, having our own exit strategies will help us to live each day more genuinely and lovingly."

Terrance W. Dushenko, PhD.
Director, Dept. of Behavioral Medicine
St. Mary Medical Center, Long Beach, CA
President/CEO, Soul Purpose and Health Psychology Associates

"From the delightful 'Bee-isms' to the profound wisdom spoken by a sage elder, author Kelsey Collins skillfully shares with us the joy of truly knowing another human being in a spiritual and intimate way. She reminds us of the often forgotten riches that reside in the beings of the elderly. Through her writing, she encourages us to 'adopt an elder' as she adopted her friend and mentor, Bee."

Ron Scolastico, Ph.D. author of *"The Earth Adventure"*
and *"Becoming Enlightened"*

"A tour de force for our time, *Exit Strategy: Leaving this Life with Grace and Gratitude,* is equally compelling as an antidote to American cultural misgivings about aging and death as it is a model for every caregiver of the elderly and dying. With deft writing, Kelsey Collins captures the psychological and spiritual processes that lead to a 'good' death. Her experiences also open avenues for reflection and discussion about how to plan for dying and death. The extraordinary examples set by the author and her elderly adoptee, Bee, will linger long after the book is closed."

Lois A. Vitt, Ph.D., Financial Gerontologist and
Editor-in-Chief of the *Encyclopedia of Retirement and Finance*

"No one knows Bee and her light and wisdom as well as Kelsey Collins. Exit Strategy captures all that is Bee and the messages she sends to the world. My own exit strategy has changed because of Bee's message and she taught me that growing old can be pretty cool."

Jerry Vaculin, Executive Director, Bishop Care Center

DEDICATION

This book is dedicated to all of us who share a common dream, to know that we are loved, free of fear or doubt, to wake up in the morning surrounded by loving friends and family, to feel honored and cherished *throughout* our lives, so that when the end of life comes we can stand on a mountaintop, open our arms and soar.

ACKNOWLEDGMENTS

More than 45 years ago I stepped cautiously into a classroom at Orangeview Junior High School in Anaheim, California. No ordinary classroom; the room was dominated by a large, fully equipped theatrical stage, complete with crimson velvet curtains and multi-colored footlights. The teacher, John Lybarger, stood behind his desk at the back of the room wearing a light pink suit and a black bow tie quietly watching his new students file into the room, their fresh, young eyes aglow at the unconventional site around them. I stuttered so badly then that I could barely get a single word out without immense embarrassment and shame, but John didn't hear my stammering; he only saw my potential, my passionate spirit, and a heart that longed to make a difference in the world. John *saw* me. John *believed* in me. He not only recognized the light in my heart, but in all of his students over a career that spanned more than 30 years.

Because of his selfless encouragement, I stood on the stage one day reading a monologue from *The Diary of Anne Frank*, a room full of kids in front of me, many of whom had teased me mercilessly every time I spit out fractured sentences. It was only John's knowing, comforting face that held me up while I read the courageous chronicles of young Anne's life. At the end of the monologue I looked out at the classroom and saw John, standing at the back of the room, tears streaming down his face. It was then that I realized that I had not stuttered – not one word – for the first time since I was four years old. Because Mr. Lybarger believed in me that day, I discovered that I could do anything, including writing this book.

And, going down the rather long list of other mentors in my life, both the supportive ones and those who presented purely difficult challenges which spurred me into making many left turns along the way, I would first like to acknowledge my mother, Ann, for her perfect demonstration of the painful consequences of keeping lifelong secrets. May your spirit dwell in eternal peace and love.

To my sister, Barbara, from the sacred protection of your bedroom when I was plum terrified as a child, to the daily motivation and support you offered as I read page after page of drafts of this book over the phone, I offer eternal appreciation and gratitude.

I have been blessed with many good, life-long friends, but none have inspired me to listen more intently to my heart than Janet, who reassures my faith in truth, and actually prefers relationships that one can chew on for a while, rather than opting for the simple vanilla pudding variety, because they're safe.

Although there were moments when I had to call in all the gods of patience, I thank my editor, Terri Daniel, for her sincere desire to make sure this book was a good read.

And, I am deeply grateful to my son, Chase, whose continued spirit guidance reminds me that I am still a mother, eternally loved by him and that an open heart illuminates all dark passages.

There are countless others, each and every one responsible for either contributing their creative spirit or giving me damn good reason to get up in the morning, and write when my mind insisted I couldn't or didn't want to. Thank you, dear ones – Bill Moss, Pamela Hunter, Dennis McGregor, Lynn Woodward, Pete Rathbun, Brent McGregor, Joe Leonardi, Lynn Talbot, Leslie Cole, Bud Hartman, Bo Powell, Brett Jarvis, Sharon Swinyard, Chris Dent, Stacey Silver, Jon Teutrine, Kay Wolf, Forrest Babcock, Bill Miller, Bruce Capitain, Keith Hofer and Marta Smith.

Finally, thank you to Bee Landis, without whom I would have remained ignorant of the plight of our elders. Your stouthearted zest for life and relentless quest to discover who we are will forever be a beacon of light as I continue on down the road for a while longer.

Until next time, oh precious friend.

Cover photo by Lynn Woodward - www.lynnwoodwarddesign.com
Back cover photo by Brent McGregor - www.rockymountaintimberproducts.com
Cover design by Pamela Hunter
Illustrations by Dennis McGregor - www.dennismcgregor.com
Interior design by Terri Daniel - www.terridaniel.com
Photo of Bee Landis by Forrest Babcock

TABLE OF CONTENTS

INTRODUCTION

If you picked up this book because you're the caregiver for an elderly parent, I thank you profoundly. Chances are you were born sometime between 1946 and 1964, making you a member of the baby boom generation (there are about 75 million of us in America, representing about 29% of the U.S. population). If you were one of the first births following World War II, you turned 60 in 2006, and if you're lucky, you might even be retired now.

Unlike your parents' generation, you may have practiced living a more conscious lifestyle by eating well, exercising regularly and seeking creative ways to manage stress. And there has probably never been a thought in your mind about the possibility of ending your days on earth in a nursing home, screaming throughout the night for help, praying that someone, anyone, will come and change your wet diaper before breakfast, or that someone, anyone, will come and visit... please.

Currently, there are approximately 1.9 million nursing home beds in the United States. It is estimated that 30% of us baby boomers will live in one for at least a portion of our lives, perhaps right when we had imagined ourselves taking a long cruise in the Mediterranean, shooting our age at golf or starting a new career doing something we really love. I defy anyone to produce a human being who dreams of spending even one day in a nursing facility, much less the last precious months or years of his or her life.

A significant percentage of our elders have limited contact with the outside world, other than the staffs of the nursing facilities in which they will spend the rest of their lives. They have no one to advocate for them and no voice of their own. There's no one to hear their lively, personal stories, to touch them or hug them, kiss them goodnight or keep them entertained and mentally stimulated. When someone – anyone – walks in to pay a visit, the sad, lonely world of nursing home residents suddenly come to life.

It takes a rare human being to lovingly care for our beloved elderly day after day. Nursing homes are plagued with staffing problems in terms of the staff numbers required and finding those who are appropriately licensed and trained. I am humbled by their service and salute them all with this book.

In the nursing homes I have visited, I was astounded to hear that nearly 30% of all the elderly patients are rarely, if ever, visited by anyone. Many sit in their rooms day after day after day, staring blankly at the television or through the window. Those who can walk slowly shuffle down the carpeted hallways, often taking twenty minutes or more to travel fifty feet.

Ask 87-year-old Bee Landis, the inspiration for this book and one of the greatest spiritual teachers of my life. She'd be the first to say she didn't much like it at the care center where she lived for four years. Not because it's a horrible place, but because there were precious few people there who shared her unusual perspective on life. The difference between Bee and many other elders was that Bee lived almost completely in the present moment. Surgery to remove a benign brain tumor in 1994 wiped out almost all of her memories, such as the memory of her wedding day or the 40 years she spent teaching children in elementary schools. Dementia pecked away bit by bit at whatever retention she had left. She has a son, but has no memory of ever making love or raising her son.

For those who believe we are the sum total of our experienced memories, that would be a sad state indeed. For Bee however, it was a perfect springboard from which to dive into her deepest feelings *right now*, in the present, because the present was all she had.

Baby boomers spend billions of dollars trying to get honest with themselves through therapy, self-help books, meditation and anything else that might provide a springboard into the present moment. We "try" to love our shadows, to live worthwhile, satisfied lives, and to be in the present moment as much as possible. For Bee, there was ONLY the present moment. Every day she saw essentially the same people coming and going at the care center. The average length of stay in a nursing facility is about 2.5 years according to current resident data, so Bee, in her fourth year as a resident, was on borrowed time. At the end of her third year, she professed wanting to live "at least five more *productive* years." Emphasis on *productive*.

Whether we like it or not, most of us are going to be old before we die. Watching our grandparents and parents grow old and lose their independence along with their eyesight, continence, cognition or hearing is a foreshadowing of what will very likely be happening to us at some point. How we boomers treat our beloved elders may someday come back and either haunt us or be pleasurably reminiscent, not as a karmic threat, but as an opportunity to choose love over fear, kindness over impatience, compassion over neglect.

When my mother was dying of fourth-stage ovarian cancer in the late 1980s, I lived with her for the last three months of her life, shooting her up daily with morphine, and connecting a liquid diet to a portacath in her chest. We would walk, when she was still able, down to a nearby greenbelt, where a row of towering gray-green eucalyptus trees stood as if tall soldiers waiting to greet us. These immense, familiar trees offered her a comforting sanctuary and respite from her painful disease. Toward the very end of her days, our last walk took three times as long to travel the short block. At one point she looked up at me and said, with tears in her eyes, "Thank you for this. Thank you for taking the time and not being in a hurry. This will come back to you someday."

Having sufficient financial resources and a loving, caring family is extremely helpful at the end of life, but for me the question is far simpler than finances or family. It's about how I want to be treated when I am old, perhaps frail and sick, and it is directly related to how I treat others now. It can be bewilderingly stressful dealing with our elders, but there is a way to transform that stress into an astonishing gift if we are willing to open our hearts to see *their* contribution to *us* as a powerful and eternally lasting exchange of the human spirit.

What you are about to read is based primarily on telephone conversations that took place between Bee and me almost daily over the course of two years. Because I can type as fast as she can talk, our two-year dialogues were typed out word-for-gloriously-funny-word, and included some jaw-dropping verbal jewels from Bee, such as *"God is SO big. How did I ever get in the position to tell God how to do anything? I feel like I'm on the crest of a wave. I'm not afraid of the storm anymore."*

3

Initially I thought the transcripts of these conversations would make a great gift for Bee's grandsons, in the hope that someday they would appreciate an enlightening glimpse into the life of their amazing grandmother. Soon, however, I realized that our conversations would be of enormous value to caregivers of the elderly. The more consistent our conversations, the more Bee opened to the marvel of her human spirit.

Our phone conversations were interspersed every six to eight weeks by in-person visits with actual "eyeball-to-eyeball" time, as Bee was fond of saying when I would make the eleven-hour drive to Bishop to spend time with her. Looking into anyone's face while talking can release a deeper range of emotions that lie just beneath the surface of our words, revealing fire-breathing dragons or the tender mews of newborn kittens. It is how we get to witness the vulnerability and the existence of authenticity in another being.

Often when Bee looked at me, her penetrating blue eyes just staring as if willing herself to climb deep down inside my soul, all I wanted to do was open myself to her, allowing her in. As a thirsty plant needs water to survive, I could feel how vital she was to me. Thus, while our telephone talk was unquestionably important, our touch-time was critical, for both of us.

Only a month before our conversations began, when I found Bee slumped over in a wheelchair in the care center, fist poised to punch me in the face, no one could have convinced me she was going to survive much longer, much less help me write this book. There are more than 20,000 books for caregivers available today, some of which I have read, and every one of them useful. But this book was created to reveal the joy that is possible for a caregiver to experience via the act of adopting an elder.

In order to be successful caregivers, we need to learn how to get more out of the care-giving experience than we put in. Bee had no idea how much she gave me during our years together, and was oblivious to the value I received from her wise and comical insights and the depth of her courage as a "spiritual spelunker." I lapped up every yummy morsel she shared with me every day, including those days when she was irate over her cold scrambled eggs or didn't remember how to use the mute button on the remote control… again.

We have a tendency to forget, perhaps purposefully, that we are all going to die someday. How we choose to live today directly affects the nature of that end zone. I have learned that we don't die any differently than we live. The two are as dependent on each other as how carefully and lovingly we tend our vegetable gardens or our automobiles.

There is an underlying gift here to show us that we are all teachers to someone in life. The moment you connect with a sad, lonely and frightened elder, you give him or her your time, your attention and your gentle touch. In this way you can open up a channel for them to contribute to *your* life in a way you never imagined possible. The days and final moments leading to our deaths can be the most important time we spend on earth, preparing us for whatever lies beyond our five senses. To participate in that time more fully, more passionately, knowing we have been loved — even by a relative stranger — can make for a lovely transition into a glorious tangerine sunset. And, when it's time to make our *own* final crossings, we'll be better prepared ourselves.

I'm in Here

Hey, *I'm in here.*
Don't you see me?
I'm the one with graying hair that
you'll get one day, too, when you get tired of the red,
or the black or the purple.
I'm the one who watches you walk by, day after day,
too busy to ask me more than a perfunctory "How are you?"
… too busy to actually stop and listen to the answer.

Hey, *I'm in here.*
Don't you hear me?
I'm the one who wants to tell you who I am,
who is calling out to you when you walk by.
I'm the one with raucous vaudeville stories,
that-day-I-hit-a-homerun-outa-the-park stories,
the you-shoulda-been-there stories
of neighborhood block parties, prize-winning fudge,
white-on-white weddings
and ex-husbands.

Hey, *I'm in here.*
Don't you feel me?
I'm the one who is just like you – only older –
and wiser sometimes,
with a heart like yours; frayed around the edges, perhaps,
but beating, nevertheless.
I'm the one who yearns to make a difference
one more time
before it's too late.

— *Kelsey Collins with Bee Landis, 2008*

6

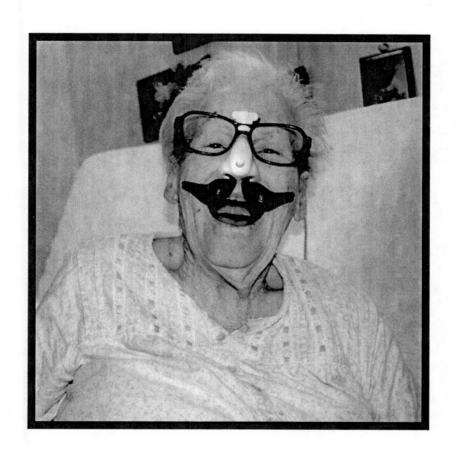

Myrtle "Bee" Landis

"I am the Bee that Bee built."

You've got something to learn in this life and God is the biggest acceptor.

1.The Wisdom of Bee

"It's like this lake here. It's been here for millions of years and yet you and I can only see the top of it. We can only see the reflection of the sky or the mountains on it. There's so much more down there we *can't* see from here. There's life there that we can only imagine. We're like that. There's so much more to us than we know."
                                                    – *Bee Landis*

She stands at the doorway, scanning the busy dining room, taking a deep breath, already questioning whether it was a good idea to leave the relative comfort of her room for lunch. Reaching down to remove lint from her dark blue pants for the tenth time, she grips the handles of her walker, carefully lifts the metal frame forward and takes a step. She notices there are seven elders seated around the taller tables against the back windows which are reserved for those who need to be fed, like babies in highchairs. Several other elders, mostly women, are being helped to their tables by nurses and other aides. A man looks over at her, briefly making cherished eye contact. She sees that as a good sign to join him at his table for lunch. Maybe today will be different. Maybe today he'll talk to her, entice her with stimulating stories and opinions. Maybe today she'll get to make someone laugh.

Instead, in the silence between her and the man, she counts the few hairs on top of his head as he looks down at his meal. Seven, eight, nine hairs, she counts to herself, wondering about male baldness and why women don't wear their hair out like men do. While waiting for lunch to be served, she fusses with the white paper napkin, folding and unfolding it, finding just the right size to fit under her sagging chin. Little disturbs her more than spilling food on the few clothes she has.

When lunch is placed before her, she grumbles to herself about the gravy smothering the piece of meat. She hates that, and has told the kitchen staff at the care center

9

many times to put the gravy on the side, but she thinks nobody listens to an old lady anyway, so why should she complain. The fact that she will spend the rest of her life in this place where relatively few listen and hardly anybody talks is a thought she can ill afford. With a deep breath of resignation she finishes her meal in silence. She remembers a quote from a time long ago: *Spiteful words can hurt your feelings, but silence breaks your heart.*

When I learned nine years ago that Bee Landis was alive, well and living at an assisted-living complex in Bishop, California, I was stunned and delighted. I couldn't wait to drive the forty-five miles through the majestic Sierra Mountain range to see her.

Standing in front of her room on the second floor, I collected myself, asking my heart to calm down a bit as I was sure it was louder than the sound of my knuckles on her door. Was it just nervousness or was it excitement about the unknown? A small tag next to the door indicated this was the right room. In the middle of the door hung a wood carving in the shape of a heart with the word WELCOME painted in shades of lavender and purple, Bee's favorite colors.

I knocked, and a booming voice from within yelled, "I'm comin'! I'm comin'!" The door opened and there she was, a face full of smiles, her short hair as bright and carrot-red as ever. "Oh, I know you, don't I?" she asked. It was very clear she didn't recognize me at all.

Little did I know then how profoundly my life would change because of this precious woman named Myrtle "Bee" Landis. An elementary school teacher for more than thirty years, Bee decided one day to take her love of teaching and her love of life to the Science of Mind church pulpit. I met her in 1982 on a Sunday morning when I walked into the small church she had started in Bishop. Bee was the minister, and "her" church, as she lovingly referred to the old storefront, brick building, was on a side street off U.S. Route 395, a highway that slices the long way through the state of California, up to Reno, Nevada and beyond to the north.

A few people were mingling inside the assisted-living facility, mostly older people, those not-so-kindly referred to as "gray-haired" by the thirty-somethings in today's society. Even though Bee was more than 60 years old at the time, she was no gray-hair, by any reference to either her hair color or her age. To call Bee's hair red would be way short of the depth and breadth of that primary color. It would be like simply calling the sun yellow. Bee's hair was fiery hot and intense; the color of ripe persimmons with a little bit of pumpkin and copper thrown in. She said she'd been dying her hair for so long she didn't remember what her natural color was.

Bee's ministry, like her personal life, was a mixture of raucous laughter and passionate (often uncomfortable) scrutiny into the personal lives of her small congregation. I attended her church somewhat regularly for several years, mostly just to hear her harmonizing at the top of her lungs: "I'M ALIVE, AWARE, AWAKE, ENTHUSIASTIC!"

Even though I was ordained as a minister in the early 1970s, I'd left my Christian beliefs behind to explore several Eastern philosophies, including Buddhism and Hinduism. When Bee discovered this, she anointed me as her "rent-a-minister," to serve in her place when she was out of town or during her infrequent bouts of illness. It was during the late 1980s that Bee proved to me, without any shred of doubt, the depth of her commitment to loving her church members by showing them the way to a deeper truth about themselves and their relationships with God.

I found myself sharing intimate details of my personal life with Bee, which at that time closely resembled a train wreck. I was sinking deeper into a loveless hell realm in my marriage, and my only son had just been discharged from the Navy with a less-than-honorable distinction, perched at the beginning of a nasty addiction to crystal methamphetamine. On top of that, my relationship with my mother was deteriorating so badly that I could barely stand to talk to her, even on the telephone.

In the spring of 1986, Bee called to say she wanted to see me, and asked if I would be willing to drive down to the Owens Valley for a chat. An hour later I was sitting next to Bee in her car as she drove out to the middle of a desolate corner of the valley, a large moraine near the Alabama Hills made famous by "B" Western movies back in the 1940s

11

and 50s. The Sierra and White Mountain ranges to the east and west were still partially covered with winter's snowy blanket. In contrast, it was nearly 80 degrees in the high desert valley, so I rolled the window down to let in some fresh air. Seeming to follow us, almost as an omen, a carefree red-tailed hawk screeched, its wingtips flared expansively like fingers as it soared effortlessly in the deep blue sky. Watching it for a while, I remembered that in the Native American tradition, among many others, a hawk is a messenger, so I wanted to pay close attention to the "Spirit Memo" I was receiving.

When I asked what in the hell we were doing out in the middle of nowhere, Bee simply smiled and said, "You'll see."

The next thing I knew, Bee took an abrupt right turn off the paved highway onto a narrow dirt road, knifing through mint-green sagebrush. I had the distinct feeling she had been there before. We drove in silence for a few miles, and the only sound was the crunching gravel under the moving tires. Eventually she stopped the car next to an enormous boulder that I thought was oddly shaped like a giant throne.

"This is it," she said. "We can get out now."

The "throne" wasn't an isolated granite sculpture in the middle of the desert landscape that I'd initially perceived. Instead, it was accompanied by several smaller boulders, almost like loyal subjects, situated in a perfect semi-circle around it, as if placed there by Spirit for just such an occasion.

"That's you, right there," Bee said pointing to one of the smaller rocks to the right of the throne. "Go over there. And don't talk.

"Now this big one here is your mother. We're not leaving here until you tell her everything you ever wanted to say but were afraid to say. Every last bit of it, you understand? We're not leaving until it's all out of you. We're miles away from anybody. No one can hear you. So, let her have it."

I would have laughed at the thought of my mother sitting on a granite throne, accepting it as perfect for her royal justifications, but it was instantly apparent that Bee wasn't in one of her humorous moods. She said she was sick and tired of me bitching about my life and not doing anything about it. She was deadly serious.

I did what anyone, face-to-face with a 5'4" parrot-red-haired-sixty-something staring at you with unyielding eyes would do; I started yelling at my mother, the Queen.

Within several minutes a few tears began to fall. Later, the screams came. After thirty minutes the tears and the screams turned into bone-numbing sobs. Just when I thought I was empty of all of it, Bee wrapped her arms around my stomach, squeezing tightly, and with of all her strength yelled in my ear, "You're not there yet. I want you to get to the part that's down HERE," emphasizing the last word in a way that took my breath away and brought me to my knees. Whatever was left inside of me came out in a steady stream of vomit. Throughout it all, Bee never left my side. When she wrapped her arms around me I felt like a little girl, probably for the first time in thirty years. I felt as free as the hawk I had seen earlier. My angry thoughts and erroneous beliefs had limited my ability to soar above my life and gain a greater perspective.

Because of that day with Bee, when my mother was diagnosed with stage four ovarian cancer in 1989, I was able to spend the last three months of her life by her side twenty-four hours a day. Because of Bee, the decaying relationship with my mother was transformed into one of loving compassion, patience and understanding. *That* was Bee.

Around 1992, Bee moved to Bakersfield with her aging mother, and took a position at the Science of Mind Church. That's when I lost track of her.

Bee was living in a nursing-care facility in her still-favorite little Western town – Bishop. I called her nearly every day since we reconnected in 1997, and during that time learned that Bee had been diagnosed with a rather large, benign brain tumor in 1994. The surgeons were able to remove about 80% of the tumor, and with it her sense of smell and the majority of her memories. That's why she seemed to not know me back in late 1996 when I knocked on her door. She said she always remembered faces though, even if she had no story-memory tagging along with the face.

After the surgery, her doctor prepared her for the likelihood that the tumor would start growing again, and that, when it did, it would be inoperable. To combat seizures – a common side effect of brain surgery – Bee was put on a combination of Phenobarbital and Dilantin, both

13

anti-convulsant medications commonly used by epileptics. By the beginning of 2004, the drugs were taking their toll on Bee's ability to have lucid conversations. Although medicated, Bee would experience what are known as "petit mal" seizures several times a week or even several times a day. These smaller seizures would manifest as "staring episodes" lasting only a minute or so, without confusion afterwards. She also began to fall regularly, fracturing both her shoulder and her elbow. Her doctor expressed concern that she may have been in the midst of a petit mal seizure during those falls, and each time, Bee had to be taken by ambulance to the hospital for an overnight stay. It was highly recommended by her doctor and assisted-living caregivers that she be moved to a new, full-care facility, the Bishop Care Center.

Bee was transferred to a double room in the care center, which resembled a more traditional hospital environment; with little room for her many personal belongings. I boxed those up so they could be transported to her son's house in Reno. The remainder I arranged in her room so they would be in place when she arrived at her new "home." I use quotes here purposefully, as I find the term "nursing home" to be often disingenuous. Some of these convalescent care facilities are little more than disinfected infirmaries where most of our precious elders will die. Unlike many nursing facilities where I have visited, often anonymously, the Bishop Care Center is one of the cleanest, cheeriest facilities I've seen and for that I am eternally grateful.

In the days following Bee's admittance to the care center, I noticed an almost daily decline in her demeanor and well-being. One day I drove down to take her to lunch, but when I arrived she was not in her room. I found her down the hall slumped over in a wheelchair, a small white pillow tucked under the right side of her body to keep her somewhat erect. Drool was oozing down her chin as she looked up at me with watery eyes. Bending down so I would be eye-to-eye with her, I said, "Hello, my darlin'," in a soft voice. She raised her fist at me, almost snarling, sounding drunk. "You are someone who says 'yes, but...' aren't you? I could just hit you." She had no idea who I was.

I leaned forward so my face was within slugging distance and said, "Go ahead, Bee. Let me have it. Right here on the kisser. It's okay. I know you love me."

Wiping her mouth slowly, she looked away as if I wasn't there. When I drove back home I had to stop on the side of the road to sob for a while, wondering if I had done the right thing by agreeing to move her into the full-care facility. The agony of knowing what to do with our aging, needy elders, wondering if we are doing the right thing, making the best choices, can be a daily haunting event in the lives of caregivers.

Our daily conversations after that became so painful for both of us that I wondered if she was near death. Silly me. One week later, the day after a frustrating phone conversation, punctuated by long sighs and awkward periods of silence, Bee called me to announce, as clear as a bell, "I'm not taking any more of those damn pills."

"What pills?"

"You know... those pills that they give me for my head. I'm not taking them anymore."

"Do you mean the Dilantin, Bee? They keep you from having seizures."

"No they don't," she declared emphatically. "I want my conscious awareness. I want that more than anything. No more pills, do you hear me?"

That afternoon I called her doctor, explaining what Bee's wishes were, adding that I supported her inner guidance. When I asked him what would happen if she went off the anti-seizure medication, he said he didn't know, adding "She'll probably have more seizures."

"Will it kill her?" I asked, not sure if I wanted to know the answer.

"No."

We agreed to wean her off the medication slowly. Within ten days, Bee and I were having forty-five minute conversations for the first time in months. We talked about God... a lot. We talked about the concept of the devil and various expressions of Christianity and the whole range of human feelings. Oh yes, we talked about *all* of our feelings.

One constant source of information we shared was the Unity Church's *Daily Word*, which we read together by phone every day. Bee still refers to Louise Hay's book, *You Can Heal Your Life*, as her "little blue bible book." The frayed book sits in the basket of her metal walker, faithfully tagging along everywhere she goes. If anyone mentions a headache or a sore back, out comes the blue book where Bee finds the

15

source and associated affirmation, whether they want it or not. She has been a true believer of Hay's ministry, referencing metaphysical solutions for physical ailments from this book for twenty years that I am aware of, maybe longer. At times, she was so clear it seemed that she was literally channeling information from a mysterious Divine Source. Even today, I'm not so sure she wasn't.

Although I know very little about Bee's early life, primarily because *she* didn't remember it, what I do know is that she was an only child. She was married, but divorced her husband when her son was quite young. A short time later, her father died. Bee's need for someone to look after her son fulfilled her mother's need to have someone look after *her*, so it was a mutually satisfying resolution to have her mother move in to provide daily home and child care while Bee fulfilled the "breadwinner" role in the family. Several decades passed this way until Bee's mother passed away. When Bee's tumor was discovered in 1994, it left her in that "who am I now?" motherless whistle-stop for the first time in 74 years.

Bee taught grammar school for 30 years. Later in her tenure many of the students in her classes were children of her alumnae. When we went out for lunch in town we would periodically come across some of these former students, who often went out of their way to remind her that she had been their favorite teacher. Because she didn't remember any of them, or any of the years she spent as a teacher, Bee used those encounters as opportunities to connect with the students from her heart rather than from old memories.

The more questions I asked Bee, the more she had to dig for answers within a relatively empty memory box. Like colorful baseball caps, we tried on every four-letter word, from love to fear – and every testy word in between. Every time I would think I had heard it all, she'd rattle my cage by talking about sex and masturbation. Sometimes I would laugh so hard she would leave me gasping for breath. She would frequently giggle hysterically at her own zaniness, grateful for the opportunity to even look into the caverns of her mind. That is why I frequently called her a Spiritual Spelunker. A *spelunker* is someone who bravely explores the interiors of pitch-black caves. Mark Twain wrote in *Innocents Abroad:* "Cave is a good word...The memory of a cave I used to know was always in my mind, with its lofty passages, its silence and solitude, its shrouding gloom, its sepulchral echoes, its fleeting lights, and more than all, its sudden revelations."

Bee's mind may not have produced solid, detailed memories of her past, but there were eighty-six years of "sepulchral echoes, fleeting lights and sudden revelations" in there. I feel thoroughly blessed to be able to share the unveiling of that unique wisdom.

Bee will not be entered into the Saints' Hall of Fame. Often she acted as irascibly as a mean, mongrel dog. No one wanted to be on the wrong side of the stick when she was in a bad mood or short-tempered or when she didn't get her bed made on time. Infrequent paranoid tendencies leaked out when Bee was fearful and grumpy. Bee would periodically accuse her nursing-home roommate of stealing her slippers or whatever else she couldn't find, only to express deep remorse later when the lost item showed up "miraculously" where she hadn't thought to look.

We are born innocent, and some of us may have the great fortune to die innocently. Bee shared this innocence with me every day. She allowed me to see into her darkest inner caves, where the not-so-pretty layers of insecurity lay. Like most everyone I know, Bee suffered bravely under the delusion that she was unworthy. She understood this delusion and laughed about it often, and yet, unlike most humans, Bee didn't try to conceal it. She held it up under a powerful microscope, painfully describing what she saw and felt before releasing it to the Divine, saying, "You got me into this mess God, now get me out of it."

Bee also had her share of genuine sparkling moments, but her treasured gifts weren't a currency to be spent at a local market; they were gifts that lasted a lifetime and beyond. "So what is authentic in you?" I asked, back at the beginning of our conversations.

"Hmmm," she pondered for a moment. "What is authentic in me is a willingness to be honest with myself now, and a willingness to see me finally, at 85 years old, as worthwhile before I die."

It escapes me now the exact moment when the focus of this book met a fork in the road. That which started as a daily dialogue intended for Bee's two grandsons as evidence of their intriguing, maddening, funny, delightful, wise-cracking grandmother, morphed into a genuine plea for others to visit a nursing home someday – soon.

Then an unexpected and even more profound force demanded a voice. It called itself "exit strategy", that process by which we can determine the precise conditions at the end of our time on earth. It's a topic that comes up regularly when I wear my hospice chaplain hat. Bee taught me that I could walk all three roads simultaneously: inspiring others to take the time to honor our elders, while encouraging them to create their exit strategies, as I carefully crafted a humble offering for Bee's two grandsons.

Death *is* an absolute legislator, but not necessarily in a morbid way. Bee casually and often shared with me some of her thoughts about death, as in this exchange that occurred in 2005...

BEE: I need to be able to hear the truth. I don't do it consciously, mostly unconsciously. Stuff opens up for me now. I think I might be dying sometimes even though I want to live another five years at least. If I am going to die, I want to learn to die better. I realize I have not been so red-hot in my life.

KELSEY: How did you realize that?

B: I feel more grown up now.

K: That's an amazing statement coming from an 84 year-old woman.

B: Almost 85. I thanked God several times in the past several days for my ailment, my illness. And I feel honest about it. I realize that I have not laid that out for approval.

K: Are you saying you want God's approval for your ailment?

B: I guess so. I need to be honest with God.

K: How does that feel?

B: Free. I feel free. I want to hang around this earth a few more years. And then I think *well Bee, nobody wants to die.* Maybe I shouldn't say that. Some people do want to die, but they don't get to go; they haven't earned it. I'm hoping I'm not earning it so well that I get it.

K: I'm going to say it again and as often as it's necessary: You're not going to die one second before you are ready.

B: Thank you for that. I really want to practice what I am preaching. Life is sweeter because of you.

Initially I thought one of my roles with Bee was to help her adjust to the reality of her death, especially when I sensed a deep fear in her about dying. When you're young, vital and fully engaged with life, death seems as far away as a distant star in an invisible galaxy. We just don't relate to it the same way an 85 year-old might, especially if they are bed-ridden or confined to a wheelchair, being fed by a sympathetic aide. One might think death would be preferable to that kind of pitiful existence, but no one really knows what someone else needs. And that has been one of the greatest endowments from Bee… to accept that she was living her life her way, in her time… not mine. She taught me to relax and allow for the preciousness of life to unfold. Neither am I here to "fix" her (or anyone else) nor help her die peacefully. We all have the potential to open to our deaths with grace and gratitude, but we also have a choice about exactly HOW we want to open to our deaths.

Naturally, I wanted to make things easier for Bee. Witnessing my mother's agonizing experience in the days leading up to her death was enough to steer me away from elder care entirely. But Bee inspired me, and she helped me recall those vexing days when I watched helplessly as my mother wretched vomit for hours following her chemotherapy treatments. She helped heal many of the emotional demons I still carried inside of me as a result of that experience. I knew my life would never be the same again the day I invited Bee, her tumor, her seizures and her cantankerous, priceless moods back into my life.

19

All we caregivers can truthfully accomplish is to learn to give care as compassionately as possible. A key to our success, like the leavening benefits of yeast in a prospective loaf of bread, is allowing ourselves to be enriched in the process.

If one of the purposes of our life here on earth is to grow psychologically and spiritually, then one way to accomplish that is to allow our hearts to grow and soften as we age. How can we do that if we allow even one of our beloved elders to be abandoned and ignored? If we are truly all one, as the spiritual masters teach, then we have a responsibility to ensure that our elders will be loved, nourished and remembered.

Author, musician and mystical astrologer Rob Brezsny wrote a particularly telling lyric in a song:

> *What is the difference*
> *Between apathy and ignorance?*
> *I don't know*
> *And I don't care.*[1]

We can always choose to do nothing in our lives. Sometimes it even works out well for us, especially if we're *consciously* choosing to not choose, also known as "removing our hands from the steering wheel," *relaxing and allowing* the next moment or phase to unfold. But when we allow ourselves to become apathetic, even when we're aware of the consequences of that action, as in the current state of our elders in this country, everyone suffers.

If we are truly one, then do we not have a responsibility to ensure that our elders will be loved and nourished and remembered by someone, even when the families or facility staff is too busy, or all their friends have already passed on?

It's one thing to be old. It's quite another to be forgotten.

---

[1] Rob Brezsny - www.freewillastrology.com/cds/

2. Exit Strategy
Part One

"Death is the most crucial moment of our lives, and each and every one of us should be able to die in peace and fulfillment, knowing that we will be surrounded by the best in spiritual care."
- **Sogyal Rinpoche,**
The Tibetan Book of Living and Dying

A soft, peach-colored light streamed through the window in my mother's bedroom; her thin, pale face illuminated in a soft glow. A few minutes earlier I'd injected another 20ccs of morphine into the porta-cath that was connected to her chest, hoping it would dull the pain in her swollen, cancer-filled abdomen. It was 1989, just a few days before her death.

As I had done every day for the previous three months, I asked her if there was anything she needed or wanted to say before she died. Normally upon hearing that question she would deftly change the subject, walk out of the room or grab the remote control to change the channel on the television, hoping I'd get the hint and drop the subject. But not this time. I sat silently with her, watching the late afternoon light traverse slowly across her bed. My mother rolled over to her side, turning her back to me. This time – for the first time in three months – she answered me.

"I just can't," she said calmly. One lone tear fell from her eye, staining the pillow where the shaft of light had moved away.

And that was that. These few words were so obviously final, clearly stating "leave me (and all of my secrets) be," that there was nothing left for me to say.

In that moment I understood that we do not die any differently than we live.

My mother had chosen a life of secrets and fear, complicated by even deeper secrets about the reasons for her fear. No one really knew her because she never trusted anyone. Sadly, I realized that she felt utterly alone most of her life, and probably even more so when she was close to death. So it did not surprise me when she fell into a deep coma the next day, one that lasted for four days, her respiration becoming slower, stopping for some seconds, then speeding up, (a process called Cheyne-Stokes breathing). That was how she ended her life on earth; unaware that her husband of 34 years was snoring next to her in bed, seemingly disinterested in her condition, or that my sister and I were gently, lovingly holding her hand and stroking her cheek during those final hours.

Thirteen years later my mother's youngest sister Wanda was also facing terminal cancer. In stark contrast to the emotional and spiritual isolation my mother created for her life and death, my Aunt Wanda's end-of-life transition was what I called a perfect "exit strategy." It flawlessly mirrored not only how she fearlessly lived her life, but how precisely and consciously she chose to end it.

A few weeks earlier Wanda had told her husband Archie that she "really didn't want to die," but that she was prepared to go if it was her time. Little did she know how quickly that time would come.

Two days before her death, I received a call telling me that the end was near and to get down to Wanda and Archie's Beverly Hills home as quickly as possible. I called my sister to tell her to fly in from her home in Oregon the next day.

When my sister and I entered their spacious house on Mulholland Drive we were met by our two female cousins, whose weak, grateful smiles were accompanied by swollen eyes from hours of crying. My uncle Archie, ever the efficient one, quietly took my sister's luggage up to their spare room, before escorting us into their bedroom to visit with our dying aunt.

Even though Wanda was on oxygen, I could see she was struggling to breathe, taking short sips of air through the cannula in her nose. Her bright blue eyes lit up when we walked to the foot of her bed, a stunning view of the Pacific Ocean clearly visible through the large windows to the west. She beckoned to all four of us, my sister, her two daughters and me, to join her on the bed.

"I'm so glad you're all here," she said weakly, her voice just barely above a whisper. "We have a movie for all of us to watch together

24

tonight. It's the new film, *Frida*, about the famous artist, Frida Kahlo. Won't this be fun?"

We all just looked at each other and giggled. This was our Wanda, a movie buff to the very end. All we needed to do was to show up with hot, buttered popcorn and she'd be happy.

Later that night we were all propped up on the bed with Wanda and Archie, watching *Frida* and eating popcorn, when she sat straight up and said, "I'm tired of this game."

For a second I wondered what game she was talking about, but the answer came quickly. "I want you all to go home to your beds so I can make my transition alone here with Archie."

At 5:30 the next morning my cousin woke me to tell me that Wanda had passed away, exactly as she had planned.

That is the difference between creating a successful exit strategy and not having an exit strategy at all.

Ever since my late teens, when I embarked on a more concerted, intent-filled spiritual practice, I'd heard from various teachers and mystics about the importance of envisioning what we want in our lives. The recent mega-phenomenon of the book and DVD *The Secret* encourages us to use everything at our disposal – from our five senses to our minds and hearts – to deeply visualize how we want to live our lives, thereby attracting what we really want. Although this news was hardly a "secret" to many spiritual seekers worldwide, it did create quite a stir in America's emerging spiritual-awareness culture. While the age-old practice of visualization is critical to creating the lives we want while we're alive, we may also want to consider using the same techniques when we are nearing the end of our time on earth.

This transition blueprint, or exit strategy, is what I discussed with Bee in October, 2006 while we were driving up the grade to Lake Sabrina in the Eastern Sierra mountain range. It was a glorious, sun-filled autumn day, clean and bright, where we were surrounded by large ponderosa pines, dark green mountain hemlocks, and fully-blossomed yellow rabbit brush; a perfectly peaceful backdrop for our conversation.

Staring contentedly at the lake's rippling surface, Bee said, "Every day I ask myself, 'Why don't I want to die?' And I answer, 'Because I don't want to go now.' There are things I want to complete before I go."

"Do you know what those things are," I asked, placing my hand on her frail shoulder.

"Yes and no," she answered, her eyes still riveted on the dancing movements across the lake. "I'm afraid to say them because if I identify them specifically, I'm afraid that'll be my push-off, and I don't want to go now."

"Declaring what you want doesn't have to mean your life will end, Bee. It's just a way to let you know what you want so you can start completing things on your list. Our fear keeps us from our joy. If we were truly living the lives we were intended to live, our lives *and* deaths would be another magical experience in a long, infinite series of magical experiences."

Bee squeezed my hand, bringing it up to her face tenderly, before continuing, shifting her gaze toward me. "Oh, well, I guess I don't know what I want."

"Do you want to know?"

"I think so."

"For me," I said, looking unwaveringly into her deep blue eyes, "every day is a good day to die."

"That's good. Maybe I can learn from you." In that moment, our eyes locked compassionately into each other, our hands entwined gently, I felt the deepest connection with Bee I think I'd ever experienced. Not two beings, but one, sharing an extraordinary moment in time.

"Perhaps we can start thinking about your exit strategy now," I said, moving my fingers lightly around the outside of Bee's ears, something my mother used to do with me when I laid in her lap as a child.

"What's that?"

"Creating exactly, precisely, how you want to make your transition, what it will look like, who is with you, and how you want to feel. Things like that. But only when you're ready."

"Okay," she said, as she watched a flock of Canada geese dip their wings over the surface of the lake, for a perfect landing. "I'll let you know."

For several weeks I broached the subject again and again with Bee during our daily telephone conversations, but each time she resisted, reminding me a bit of my mother's counteraction game. This time however, I was resolute, because I trusted Bee when she told me about her desire to live as consciously as possible. During one conversation, when her voice was amazingly clear, she told me that facing her own death directly was a part of that consciousness practice.

B: I want to die dead.

K: Please tell me more about that.

B: I want to be sure when I die that I have used it all up. Does that make sense?

K: Absolutely.

B: I want to be sure that I'm dead when I die. I want to do it on purpose. I want to live on purpose too. You know that word, consciousness? Well, I'm just beginning to understand what it means. My life is getting better all the time. It's interesting and I am so happy to be here now. I want to be equally conscious when I die.

K: Being here now is the whole game, Bee, no matter what age we are. Is it time to talk about your exit strategy now?

B: (hesitating) I think so.

K: Let me know when you are sure, okay?

Bee seemed to want to change the subject after that, but agreed that we would talk about it more fully during our next eyeball-to-eyeball visit. This is not uncommon, this distracting, switching-subjects ploy, both on the part of the elder and the caregiver. Because we often tend to trivialize death, we may feel invaded when the subject is introduced. It takes artful perseverance, patience and trust for both the dying one and the caregiver to have a comfortable, conscious conversation about death.

Many people die unprepared for death in much the same way they may have lived unprepared for life.

According to the online encyclopedia *Wikipedia*,[2] the definition for exit strategy is: "*a means of escaping one's current situation, typically an unfavorable situation. An organization or individual without an exit strategy may be in a quagmire. At worst, an exit strategy will save face; at best, an exit strategy will peg a withdrawal to the achievement of an objective worth more than the cost of continued involvement.*"

The term is most commonly used in military jargon or in the corporate world. In the case of our current political administration, President George W. Bush has been publicly derided for not having an exit strategy for the war in Iraq, but by any definition, planning how to exit your business world (or your life) is just as important as planning how to enter it. According to many of the Eastern philosophies, the moments just prior to death may be even more critical than all of the millions of moments that came before, and the quality of one's death may be even more important than the quality of one's life.

In American culture we tend to see death as something to be avoided at all costs, as if dying represents some sort of failure or weakness. One of the most complete and authoritative books ever written on death is Sogyal Rinpoche's *The Tibetan Book of Living and Dying*. Written in 1992, it has sold more than a million copies worldwide and has been translated into more than 20 languages. It is a remarkably accessible book that speaks to people of all faiths and traditions, encouraging compassionate care and love for the dying. As if speaking directly to my heart, Rinpoche asked in the book, "Isn't it terrifying that we discard old people when their working life is finished and they are no longer useful? Isn't it disturbing that we cast them into old peoples' homes, where they die lonely and abandoned?"

Several years ago I initiated a conversation about graceful passages with my aging stepfather who'd been suffering from the effects of a severe right-brain stroke for nearly 17 years. A stubborn, despondent man in general, with decades of pent-up anger stored beneath the surface of his weathered face, he could no longer walk or feed himself, and was

---

[2] www.wikipedia.org

confined to a wheelchair which embittered him even more. To make matters worse, he had been recently diagnosed with a slow-growing lung cancer. The day I drove down to Southern California to visit him, I brought along a CD entitled *Graceful Passages*,[3] an encouraging and inspirational mixture of beautiful music and wisdom-filled insights on death from well-known mystics and masters from universal faiths.

Before I left I called to ask if he needed or wanted anything, remembering how much he loved hamburgers. As if reading my mind, he answered "A hamburger from the In-and-Out place would be nice." When I walked into the house, the bag of fast-food clenched in my fist, my stepfather was sitting in his wheelchair at the kitchen table facing away from me. It was shocking to see how much weight he'd lost. His 6'2" frame was now shriveled and skeletal, curled into itself to the point where he could only look down at his lap. I carefully fed him the treasured burger and fries, but if I wanted to make eye contact with him I had to get down on the floor and look up into his face.

His live-in aide, an older Armenian man, was blithely talking about their recent visit to the oncologist, who'd told them that my stepfather could easily live another two years. My stepfather's groan was audible. "How do you feel about that?" I asked as I picked up a French fry that fell out of his mouth.

"I think that sucks," was his curt reply.

"You know," I said, looking deeply into his watery blues eyes to see if he was listening, "you can choose to let go." It took a few moments for him to chew on his food before he could respond.

"What in the hell are you talking about? How do I do that?"

"Just choose to let go. Our ability to choose is our greatest strength."

Although he didn't have much more to say about it, I sensed that he'd heard me on a deeper level, and that it was time for me to go. When I approached the front door I paused for a moment to hear a particularly moving passage I remembered from the CD by Rev. Alan Jones, an Episcopal priest, emanating from the living room.

---

[3] www.gracefulpassages.com/

"In my tradition we try to practice dying every day so that we may be fully alive. What I understand of my prayer life is to place myself on the threshold of death, to participate in my dying, so that I may live each day and each moment as a gift. What I cultivate is a grateful heart; each moment then becomes a new thing. My gratitude comes from the sheer gift of life itself."

Promising to stay in touch, I said goodbye to my stepfather for the last time. Two weeks later I received the midnight call informing me that he'd passed away. According to his aide, he had listened to *Graceful Passages* every day, and in the end he seemed to be very peaceful. I believe it was the first time in his 74 years on earth that my stepfather had consciously chosen anything. I couldn't think of a better moment to start, and although he may have not consciously chosen an exit strategy, he did allow for the possibilities to penetrate through the insights of the wise ones in *Graceful Passages.*

Reflecting on that time with my stepfather, I realized that it was time for us to get down to the business of creating her exit strategy. A few weeks later the opportunity presented itself when I drove down to Bishop to spend some one-on-one time with my engaging, aging friend.

When I walked into Bee's room I found her fully dressed but asleep on her bed, breathing heavily. Even though I said my traditional "Hellooooooooooo Bee!" she was so deeply asleep that she didn't respond. All of her red hair was gone then, replaced by short wisps of white in a female version of a boy's, butch haircut. It made her look perky and was certainly easier for her to manage. When I bent down to arouse her, I could see the two surgical indentations in her skull where her tumor had been removed years before. They were almost the width of my thumb and about a half an inch deep, something that regularly worried Bee as she was concerned "my brains might fall out or something." Skillfully allaying those fears became a twice-monthly game between us, ranging from the deadpan, "It is impossible for your brains to fall out."... to the ludicrous, said with arching eyebrows, "I'd love it if you lost some of your brains. That way I'll be smarter than you." She especially laughed at that idea and then promptly forgot what we were talking about.

30

"Oh," she said as I lightly kissed her forehead, "You're here. I was just dreaming about you. We were on a boat on a lake and neither of us had a paddle."

A perfect segue to the exit strategy discussion.

K: (laughing) Without a paddle? It sounds like we weren't very well prepared, were we? Exactly why having a fully prepared exit strategy is a good idea, don't you think? Are you ready to tell me all about your perfect exit strategy now?

B: Yes. I've been thinkin' about it for several days. I don't want to be a pain in the ass.

K: Okay. Duly noted. But that's what you *don't* want. It's better if you create what you *do* want. Close your eyes and tell me what you see.

Bee closed her eyes for a moment, but then quickly opened them again. She looked around her room, stopping to look at the photographs of her family on the wall and then softly touched the purple, flannel quilt on her bed that she loved so much. Letting go of attachment to our loved ones and material possessions is one of the final hurdles to making a peaceful transition.

B: I'm here, in this place, of course, not in the hospital. And I'm in this bed. You and Larry aren't here. I've had a wonderful day where I feel really good, no sickness or anything. And I'm asleep, I think. It happens real quick. (pausing) And, I want no one, including me, to suffer.

K: Are you alone then?

B: No. My girls (the CNAs) are here. The ones who get along with me. The ones who really like me; they're here. *(Smiling now)* All I feel is peace... and no regrets. Not one.

K: Anything else?

31

B: What else is there?

At that point Bee stood up, adjusted her purple sweatshirt (the one that says *"I'm Adorable... and That's Enough"* on the front), and without another word wrapped her arms around me, giving me the hug that I suspect *she* needed.

There wasn't anything more for me to say or add. That was clear. Her exit strategy, like much of her life, was short and to the point. She was using her life, everything she'd learned from a large collection of spiritual books, her close friends, the kids in her classroom and her beliefs, both new and old, to prepare for her death. At this moment, the mysterious unknown, that which happens after her death, was of no concern to her. The actual process of "seeing" her transition so clearly allayed all of her fears of what lay beyond.

That was Bee's exit strategy. It seemed unfair to ask something so vitally important of Bee that I was not willing to do myself.

We feel badly when we're judged and it's only because we agreed with it, and then we get pissed.

3. Children... Woe is Them

"Children begin by loving their parents; as they grow older
they judge them; sometimes, they forgive them."
– Oscar Wilde

"I am the Bee that Bee built."
– Bee Landis

This is a plea to those of you who are willing caregivers and are *unrelated* to the elders in nursing facilities. You are pure and pristine, without the emotional baggage that family members often carry. You are in a unique position to step up and offer your time and appreciation to a fellow — often very wise — soul.

I do not presume to judge adult children who have chosen for one reason or another to disengage from their aging parents or grandparents. I want to support rather than dampen their spirits and I want to inspire rather than shame them. If, after reading this chapter on wayward family members, you find yourself feeling dishonored, please accept this as encouragement rather than judgment, and allow yourself to look intensely into the shame to discover its true source. Be kind to yourself, and consider the wonder-filled possibilities that may await you when you allow your elders to share their thoughts, fears and frustrations, even if they end up sharing these things with someone other than *you*.

Like many of you, I did not experience a successful childhood. Neither my mother nor my stepfather was a safe or loving bastion upon whom I could count as a child, and violent traumas occurred as regularly as the daily bakery truck deliveries. It was not easy to listen to the constant drumming of criticism, regret and resentment that filled my head as a young adult; yet blaming my parents for my multiple shortcomings, once an adult myself, never felt quite right to me. Not that I didn't do my share of finger-pointing. Instead, I simply noticed early on that the more I impugned my parents, the more my life fell apart. There was just no satisfaction in it for me.

While Bee was in the care center, I would witness frequently – with considerable concern – her frustrations about her only son, Larry. A year younger than I, Larry did what he could for his mother when she was hospitalized for her brain tumor. No longer mobile or able to care for herself on her own in the months following her surgery, Larry made an understandable decision to move Bee to an assisted living facility in Bishop, the town where she had lived for over thirty years. Larry's choice to move her there hinged on his notion that Bee still had friends in the area who would stop by to visit periodically.

Although Bee had a telephone installed in her room, she told me that Larry rarely called her, and that his visits were few. Many months would pass between the family visits that she so deeply cherished.

On the walls surrounding Bee's bed were dozens of photographs of Larry, his wife and their two sons, Michael and Andy. In the photographs, her "boys", as she lovingly referred to them, are dressed in sports uniforms, complimented by dark blue baseball caps, wooden bats and other equipment. Their broad smiles reveal two happy, healthy kids.

Over the years her grandsons had given her smaller photographs with little speakers built into the frames that, when touched, would broadcast the boys' voices saying, "Good morning, Grand Bee. I love you." She played these over and over again, every day, sharing them with everyone who came into her room.

Bee shared some of her hopeful, yet pain-filled feelings with me one afternoon after a long period of time had elapsed with no contact from Larry.

BEE: I made up my mind that I'm going to contact my family this weekend. I want to speak to my grandsons again. I don't know why I keep putting it off, because I look at their pictures every day.

KELSEY: Why do you think you keep putting it off?

B: I think that *they* ought to contact *me* and say hello.

K: Well, you can wait until they contact you, which might be a long time. Or you can let that go and call them. What does your heart tell you?

B: My heart says that I want to talk to my grandsons. Ooh, I just got a chill-thrill ("chill-thrills" are Bee's version of goose-bumps). That must be the truth.

Frequently, Bee's initial agitation led to what was truly bothering her, but sometimes I had to tread through a minefield to get to the source of what was troubling her. A few days after the conversation about calling her grandsons, she shared the following, after giving me a piece of her mind when I forgot to bring her new reading glasses as I had promised:

B: You're a person who is real busy with thinking all the time. So I haven't said things. I haven't wanted to make you think I'm unhappy.

K: Are you unhappy?

B: Only when it comes to my blue book, my Louise Hay bible, when I want to read something about how I can heal my eyes.

K: Is that what you're unhappy about, not being able to read?

B: But, we've said this before.

K: Oh, I see. You're talking about a while back when we said we would get you some new glasses and it didn't happen, right?

B: I'm called trouble. I don't like to ask.

K: But then you won't get what you want, right?

B: Right. I have to learn to ask for what I want. (hesitating)... A word in defense of Larry. I didn't think I was of any importance to him. Did I tell you this? The few times I called him, I left a message. When he knew it was me it made me feel good. I want to believe that he really does care. I began to realize this with my Louise Hay tapes. I haven't listened to them with an open heart. Likewise, I haven't given Larry an opportunity to be close.

K: Why do you think that is?

B: It doesn't matter. I'm not so wrapped up in the whys anymore.

K: I understand. Do you want to change that?

B: Absolutely. I want to feel comfortable around him. It's all a matter of feeling, isn't it? He's relieved, I think.

K: That must be of some comfort to you, too.

B: Yes. I will call now every once in a while. I thought it was *his* responsibility to call *me*. That's bullshit. That's ridiculous.

The next day Bee dove deeper into her feelings about her son, revealing a fractured part of her, hidden beneath layers of an unknown past. Missing him and her grandsons was to be a continued theme in our conversations. It was my sense that Bee, similar to many of the elders in these facilities across the country, felt helpless, lonely and bored. Contact with family is usually the only connection many elders have with their previous, self-determined worlds.

B: I'm feeling closer to Larry now since we've both grown up, I think. He's letting me know he has feelings for me.

K: Have you spoken to him since you called yesterday?

B: No, I don't think so. I have looked at things between us and thought, well Bee, *why don't you admit it*? I have kind of enjoyed having him looking like the dirty bum.

K: By dirty bum, do you mean for not participating much in your life now? Is that true?

B: I think so, but I don't choose to keep it anymore.

K: That's how our life changes for the better, isn't it... choosing to let go of beliefs that are no longer useful?

B: I'm willing to let it go. I can look at it now and think it wasn't such a good idea. I've let it run my life, obviously, because I suffered the results of it and I think (Larry) has, too.

What Bee taught me that day was astounding in its honesty. Without many memories of her past, Bee had no idea if she was a good mother, a bad mother, a neglectful mother or a shining example of motherhood. For some, that loss of memory might be a blessing. While Bee couldn't remember if she got up every morning to make a nutritious breakfast for her son, she did seem to have deep emotional memories, such as occasional inklings of guilt or hints of some possible negativity somewhere in her past. Naturally, mothers (and fathers) experience guilt periodically as we wind our way through the parenting highway, but most of us can attach it to a real, physical memory, but Bee didn't have that luxury.

This raises an interesting question: In the minds of their children, how long are elders given to "pay for" their transgressions in parenting? Are we using our childhood pain to shield our hearts from receiving extraordinary gifts from our elders as they near the end of their time on earth? And is that same pain preventing us from *giving* end-of-life gifts to our elders when they need them the most?

These questions, among many others, started to crop up inside my head when Bee and I began our daily dialogues. Knowing how important it was for her to have regular contact with her family, I could only hope that her son would step up to the plate and participate more in her life. There was no way that I could possibly know what was in Larry's mind, *or* his heart, with regard to his mother, or whether "stepping up to the plate" was even an option for him. In the meantime, I began an amazing journey with Bee, one in which I climbed into a cavernous and oddly surprising understanding of who *I* am.

I figure that God did not lead me this far to dump me into trouble.

4. Pity vs. Love

"Self-pity is our worst enemy, and if we yield to it,
we can never do anything wise in this world."
– Helen Keller

"Pity gives agreement to the condition you are pitying."
– Bee Landis

About a year into our dialogue, I noticed that Bee used the word "pity" repeatedly in our conversations... pitying others for what they did or didn't do, or wanting to receive more pity for herself. In Bee's day, offering pity was considered to be an act of kindness toward another. Today however, especially when directed toward oneself, it can be an act of derision and egocentricity.

As a casual suggestion, I asked Bee what pity meant to her. She told me she'd think about it and let me know. When I called the next morning, she answered the phone after a delightful morning whirlpool bath, prescribed to help with a terrible skin irritation that wasn't responding to topical medication.

BEE: I just walked into my room stark naked. Well, a towel is wrapped around me. I had a revelation during the night, and I'm trying to hold the bath towel on while I read from my yellow pad. At the top of the sheet I wrote "pity vs. love." I've been trying to love me for over 80 years but I haven't done a good job at it. I don't know how it finally dawned on me. I don't have any trouble with pity.

KELSEY: Pity is often fear-based, and it can be dis-empowering. But compassion and empathy are based in love, which is empowering. We can have compassion for ourselves and others when we sense we are hurting or frightened. We can empathically feel into another's heart. Tell me what you see.

B: *(reading from her notes)* Pity creates itself. How does it do that? We learned that we create what we receive in life. We created all of it. I have had no problem pitying people. I haven't realized that I haven't been able to love them when I do that. I pitied them instead. Of course, I didn't call it pity then. I wasn't aware of it being pity, but it was. I know that now. There isn't anything else but love.

K: This is exciting, Bee.

B: I impressed me. I thought, well, Bee, you ought to be impressed with yourself. It's taken you almost 85 years to be here. My parents thought they were doing everything right. I think they never gave me the kind of attention that I needed, but that's okay. They were doing what they were able to do. And they probably came from parents where there were sad problems, who probably didn't give them attention they needed either.

K: Do you think we can stop the flow of sadness that results in not getting our needs met?

B: When we get treated in an unkind way – at least it seems unkind to us – when we are feeling hurt, instead of condemning that person, we can simply say, well, they were treated in an unkind way, and not take it personally.

K: I would call that empathy. That's offering compassion, isn't it?

B: When I do that, I don't feel hurt anymore. So, I got to thinkin', *what's life all about*? I think life is for learning how to be creative with what we've got. It's okay to feel sorry for people who are down and out but not pity them. Pity is to give agreement to whatever the condition is that you are pitying.

K: That feels like truth, Bee.

I've had my fair share of pity-pot moments when all I wanted to do was turn out the lights, climb into the nearest toilet, and close the lid. But listening to Bee's honest perspective stirred something in me that initially felt like shame. How could this woman, almost into her ninth decade on earth, have been so positive, day in and day out, when her situation didn't change much within the four white walls around her? Let me give you a peek into what Bee's surroundings were so you understand what I'm talking about.

One entered the room through an oversized, wide door, similar to those in regular hospitals that allow beds to be moved easily in and out. An empty, fully-made bed was on the right, waiting to become home to the stranger who would become Bee's next roommate. With resignation, Bee called them her "roomies," as if she were living in a college dorm. A few feet away next to a small window was Bee's bed, covered by a purple flannel quilt, which was soft to the touch and which Bee adored. Hanging from the ceiling and around both beds, again similar to those found in regular hospitals, were pink curtains on chains for privacy. Two small wooden cabinets, two and a half feet wide, held hanging garments, shoes and slippers. As for the rest of her clothing, she normally used one of the three-drawer chests supplied, providing she didn't have a roomie. What was left of her private life before her tumor surgery, mainly photographs of her family and her certificate as a minister with the Science of Mind Church, were displayed on top of the chests and all over the walls around her bed. Without a roommate she could spread out a bit more. Not having a roommate was a good thing for Bee most of the time; she preferred her privacy, even with the consequent loneliness.

When Bee said "you've got to learn to be creative with what you've got," she wasn't just giving lip-service. To put that in another perspective, think of a time when you were in a hospital for a few days. Remember the constant noise, the constant interruption, the clatter of food trays being delivered out in the halls, and how much you wanted to get the hell out of there? Every time I walked into Bee's room I thought about my own rare experiences as a hospital patient. I was thankful for the medical help, but at the same time hated every minute of it. After a few days I always got to go home to the privacy of my own environment and my own bed.

Bee *was* home, just like the other seniors around her. Unwilling to stay in her distinctive pity-pot for longer than necessary, Bee taught me, through unflinching example, how one can use inner power and intent – to make lemonade out of sour lemons, even in the dreary monotony of a nursing facility. She was unwilling to accept anything else. For Bee, every day became a colossal cheesecake just waiting to be devoured.

Continuing our earlier conversation about pity vs. love:

B: If life here was all perfect to begin with, what's the point in living? I love to learn.

K: And look what you're learning!

B: I don't think I have to start from scratch. I just woke up excited this morning. I went down to the dining room late but it didn't matter to me. I could stand a cold breakfast. I didn't have to fuss. I didn't need to ask for my breakfast to be heated over. It didn't matter. I thought, *here I am, standing on the shoulders of yesterday, so what am I going to do about it?* I felt a day older – at least a day older. I don't want to waste that learning. I discovered I was having those seizures about every thirty days. I don't think I'm going to be having them anymore. There I was feeling *sorry* for me, because I thought that unfair things were *happening* to me; that people were looking down on me. But they weren't looking down on me. I was feeling pity from people and then I thought, *why do I need pity?* I'm getting what I think I need and if I'm getting some pity, okay, I accept it. And I've had enough of it.

A wonderful quote from Maya Angelou came to mind when Bee was sharing her feelings about feeling sorry for herself: *"Self-pity in its early stages is as snug as a feather mattress. Only when it hardens does it become uncomfortable."*

Bee wavered back and forth in terms of personal insights into her beliefs and behaviors. One day she was full of awareness and the next day her awareness retreated into the murky depths of her mind. I can relate to that perfectly. One day I'll feel as if I have an inside track to the

Universal Mind, to Divine Intelligence where everything makes perfect sense and all is in Divine Right Order. The next day I could swear the Clever Mind Bandit swept into my bedroom during the night and stole all of that conscious awareness I was experiencing the day before. Tricky bastard.

What continues to be encouraging for me as I listened to this plucky spelunker was that she kept stretching and opening up to the possibilities, even at a late stage of her life. She didn't use her age as an excuse to give up or to settle, as evidenced in this dialog:

B: What do you think about forever?

K: Forever? Infinity? Whew! It's been said that it's not only hard to think about, but harder than we can think.

B: I want to say it's all right. You can't change infinity. The point is that I keep trying to think about *now* or *forever*. Maybe they're the same thing. My mind can understand the *now* part. But I can't handle forever. I think, *Bee that's ridiculous.* So I just have to trust God.

K: Something tells me that the understanding doesn't come from a place in our mind. It comes from a place more mystifying than that; from the deepest spaces in our heart where our soul dwells.

B: I say, *You have to take over, God. I can't handle this by myself anymore.* (laughing). Oh, shit... or, uh shoot. I've been shaping up my language lately, being more dignified. I'm getting all the time that the earth is a "being." No beginning and no end. It's almost impossible for me to comprehend.

K: Keep comprehending, Bee. Keep looking. Keep asking. Keep pondering the imponderable. That's most of the game, anyway, don't you think?

B: Oh, yes. Life just keeps opening up all the time.

Our elders don't want our pity; they want our precious time and they want it consistently. They want to be heard, just like every other human being, and they want to feel valuable, just like you and I do.

How we spend the end of our lives here on earth, according to Buddhist philosophy, is critically important even if one doesn't believe in reincarnation. Allowing self-love to replace self-pity would be a huge, satisfying achievement in anyone's life. There is a misconception that caregivers take control of an elder's care, but the truth is that elders work with us in *partnership*. It takes true courage to surrender one's privacy and self-sufficiency to an altered life within the insipid confines of a care center. It's our wholehearted applause that will let our elders know that we not only celebrate their achievements, but that we affirm their endurance as a fellow human being.

Life is really interesting. If you don't like it, you're in the wrong place.

5. R-E-B-E-L

"You don't go to a department store and just stand there waiting for
someone to bring you what you want.
You have to let someone know. If you want makeup
you don't go to the hardware department and wait for them to offer you
cupcakes. You go where you want to get what you want."
– **Bee Landis**

Thirty years separated Bee and me. When she was born in 1920, the
world had just finished a war that was given the curious oxymoron of
"The Great War," and the average life expectancy was around 54 years.
The Roaring 20s was all about jazz and dancing until you dropped, and
selling liquor was a crime. The radio was becoming a familiar voice in
living rooms across the country, women were not equal to men
according to the U.S. Supreme Court, and the whole country told Emily
Post that she was the authority on proper manners by making her a best-
selling author. Commercial airlines wouldn't be in full operation until
1939, and if one traveled from California to New York it would take
more than 13 days. The continuing debate over Divine Creation vs.
evolution was brought to the national arena with the Scopes Monkey
Trial. Then, as now, certain traditionalists were afraid of losing their
ability to dictate proper American values to the rest of society. It was not
a good time to be an intellectual.

Sometime back then, Bee decided to become her version of a rebel
and a radical thinker. When still a child, she changed her name from
Myrtle to Bee after her father told her he felt as if he'd been stung the
day she was born. Most children would have shrunk off into a corner
hearing that kind of mean-spirited statement from a parent, but Bee said
she rather liked the idea of stinging people "if it makes them think."

I know only a few details about her early years, other than that she
was an only child, born in Cincinnati, Ohio, who moved with her family
to San Diego, California when she was quite young. When I met Bee she

51

was almost 65 years old and nearing mandatory retirement age as a primary school teacher. How she became interested in the Science of Mind religion is also a mystery.

The first Sunday I walked through the front door of the little church, Bee was standing inside greeting a small group of people. I don't think I'd seen hair that dazzling shade of red since Lucille Ball graced the covers of fan magazines when I was a kid. Just like Lucy, Bee would consider it a bad day if she didn't make someone laugh. Especially in church.

One of Bee's songs, which we sang regularly at her church, had these catchy, uplifting lyrics:

I'm alive, awake, aware, enthusiastic...
I'm alive, aware, awake, enthusiastic.
I'm alive, aware, awake. I'm awake, aware, alive.
I'm alive, aware, awake, en-thu-si-as-tic!

We'd sing it three times in a row, each time faster than the last. At the end of the song, Bee's face was nearly as red as her hair, and her eyes were aglow with fiery energy. Bee would make a peculiar sound at the back of her throat when she sang... *kkrrchk*, like the sound one makes when stepping on a twig. During her time at the care center we'd often sing that song together and she'd punctuate the end of it with the same sound – *kkrrchk* – as if she were back in church with her lively congregation.

It's amazing what the mind remembers. Because the brain remembers music as three different aspects (rhythm, melody and harmony) using both left and right hemispheres of the brain, someone with severe dementia can remember long-forgotten lyrics to a favorite song.[4] Bee proved that to me when she sat in my truck one day and listened to the 1940s station on the satellite system as we drove into town. I listened to her just crooning away to The Mills Brothers hit,

---

[4] This Is Your Brain On Music - *The Science of a Human Obsession*
   by Daniel J. Levitin

You're Nobody Till Somebody Loves You, remembering all the harmonies, and almost every lyric.

> BEE: People stare at me when I sing. My goal is to make them at least smile. The dining room was packed today, and I told them, *My goal is to make you guys smile.* And they just looked at me, cracks forming on the sides of their mouths. *Well, that's something,* I said. And then I told God, *You send me to the table that needs me.* And then I relax and follow God's pushes.

Bee was given the moniker, "rebel," by the care center's activity director in 2004. Every time Bee and I came across that tall, energetic blonde, she would smile and yell out to Bee, "Uh-oh, here comes the rebel rouser." The online Urban Dictionary[5] defines *rebel rouser* as *"someone who wreaks havoc; a badass."* The mere mention of the word "badass" would send Bee into fits of laughter, where she'd announce triumphantly, "You bet I am, and proud of it, too."

During one of my visits with Bee at the care center I invited a videographer friend to join me so we could capture her on video. I thought it would be a wonderful gift to her grandsons who were quite young when she had her tumor removed and hadn't spent much time with her in the ensuing twelve years. She was cheerfully waiting for us when we walked into her room, all dressed in shades of blue from her socks to her tee-shirt, wearing extremely dark sunglasses and sporting one of her favorite props, a fake arrow through her head. My friend suggested we begin shooting outside on the care center's patio where the light was a bit better than it was in her room.

Opting for her walker rather than her wheelchair, Bee decided to lose the arrow "so I won't scare my grandsons," and then led us slowly through the door, camera rolling, following her down the hallway. She was in the middle of a lively commentary on why people get sick when we were joined by two of her favorite nurses, both of whom said that Bee was the funniest, wittiest patient in the care center.

---

[5] www.**urbandictionary**.com

On one occasion Bee and I were in deep conversation about dying when a man came in to give her a necklace he'd repaired for her.

BEE: I've been thinking the past few weeks, *Bee, maybe you're dying.* But I'm not ready to go yet. I have to be willing to play the game with the right rules. The rules are you've got to be willing to look at what you're carrying. I don't want to be carrying unforgiveness in my heart (after pausing to accept the necklace from the man). Do you know what it says on my necklace?

KELSEY: No, but I bet you're going to tell me.

B: It says (spelling it out) R-E-B-E-L. Rebel

K: Fits you perfectly. Where did you get that?

B: We have a once-a-month sale here. People can donate things and we can buy things. So I bought that for myself. I found out why they got rid of it, because it was broken.

K: And the kind man fixed it for you?

B: Yeah. People are good to me. They tell me I'm a pain in the neck but they love me anyway. I want to release people that I think have hurt me because I realize I'm the only one who received the hurt (laughing). They don't believe they're really giving me pain. And I find myself closer to relaxing and smiling and letting it go (laughs louder). I know I'm not a loser because I'm not fighting for anything. I don't have to fight because I haven't lost anything. It's interesting, isn't it?

K: You are on a roll here, Bee. Keep going.

B: All I know is that I'm sort of unusual in the dining room. People kinda look at me, like, "huh?"

K: Perhaps they're wondering what planet you're from.

B: Yeah. How come she's so damned happy? Doesn't she have any sense? If she had any brains she'd know she should be miserable (laughing hysterically now). I just look at them and say, *It's a brand new day, never been used before. BRAND NEW!* That gets them every time.

As any spiritually-motivated rebel rouser would do, Bee considered it her duty to encourage deep thinking from every unsuspecting passerby. I ought to know; she gently shoved it down my throat for nearly 25 years. The power of forgiveness is high on her list of must-dos before she dies.

B: Forgiveness. Now there's a squirmy word. Everyone knows that forgiveness is something that noble people, nice people and good kids all know we should strive for. It is probably number one on everyone's "should-do" list. *The Course in Miracles*[6] tells us that every illness we have is based on an unforgiveness of someone or something. But I doubt many of us can believe that until we prove it in our lives. Well, what is forgiveness? It would seem to me it's getting rid of a hurt that we have carried around within us; perhaps for a long, long time. But why have we carried it within, never quite letting it go? It seems to me the answer to that is because I don't deserve to let it go or I don't deserve to be forgiven.

There were many times that my imagination, helped by knowing this woman-sage, would allow me to see Bee's face when she and I would talk on the telephone. I could see how the corners of her eyes looked like hairline cracks in concrete when she squinted at me when emphasizing something she was saying. Sometimes, when she wanted to make an even bigger point, she'd purse her lips together for emphasis,

---

[6] www.courseinmiracles.com/

like Betty Boop. I imagined her just like that as she continued her diatribe on forgiveness, using constipation and crap as a metaphor:

> B: Well, what is forgiveness? Nature has a wonderful way of separating living material from what's no longer necessary for a vibrant, healthy life; whether it's dead leaves or something that was once green and beautiful. Well, what about our physical bodies? We eat food that nourishes us, and when we have received energy and growth from it, it changes form and is released from our bodies, and that is called defecation or bowel movements or, in street language, *shit*. It's hardly anything nasty or filthy. It just isn't necessary anymore. And we certainly don't hang on to it. We joyfully let it go, especially if we've been constipated for a while. Not so easy to let go of the mental junk, though, is it? Forgiveness is the willingness to let go of all that mental junk that has gotten in the way of loving each other. It's as simple as that. The Bible says, in Proverbs 23:7, "As a man thinketh in his heart, so is he."

> K: That worketh for women, too!

> B: So I'm really concerned what I'm carrying in my heart today. And what I no longer have "useth" for, I'm letting it go. Thank you, God, for a clean mind. Now I want a clean heart.

> K: I am breathless. That is extraordinary, Bee.

> B: Is it? Do you think it will work in our book?

> K: Of course.

> B: Oh, good. I wanted to leave a mark.

After many conversations with Bee, I've decided why the name R-E-B-E-L is so appropriate for her. It stands for Rambunctious Endearing Bee Enters Life—in her time and in her way.

I'm beginning to realize that I'm contaminating what I see with my own contaminating thoughts.

6. Rule Number Six

"After God created the world, He made man and woman.
Then to keep the whole thing from collapsing,
He invented humor."
– Guillermo Mordillo, cartoonist and animator

"I don't think that anything that happens to us is
permanently implanted. It just passes through."
– Bee Landis

In the early months after Bee settled into the care center, I brought a large, colorful poster to display on the closet door directly across from her bed where she could easily read it. In large red letters, it said:

RULE NO. 6:
DON'T TAKE YOURSELF SO DAMNED SERIOUSLY

I had just finished reading Wayne Dyer's inspirational book, *The Power of Intention*, and so loved the simple canon of Rule No. 6. [7]

Generally, I laugh more than most people do and even more so now as a result of my relationship with Bee. Seriousness has tension as its main component, which is not exactly an open conduit for the flow of positive energy. It's impossible to be serious and cheerful at the same time, evidenced by these synonyms for "serious" in the dictionary: *austere, weighty, deadpan, stern, downbeat, draggy, severe, unsmiling,* and *funereal.* Makes you want to run right out and take the seminar on how to be more serious, doesn't it?

---

[7] Please see page 149 for an explanation of Rule Number Six

Last time I checked there were over 200,000 books on achieving a joy-filled life, and more than 63 million Websites devoted to happiness.

What does this tell us, and what is Bee telling us? The first thing Bee does when I call in the morning is to giggle. And then we sing the "Alive, Aware, Awake" song, real loud, as if no one but us are listening. I don't know about you, but I'll take bliss, cheerfulness, contentment, ecstasy, enchantment, jubilation, merriment and well-being any day.

Why are we so friggin' serious, I wonder? Even the fact that I choose "friggin" instead of the other "f" word is evidence of our habitually humorless nature. I realize that some words are offensive to some people, but why? Is it political correctness, old-fashioned Puritanism, or a form of self-righteousness? They are just "bloody words," as Bee often reminds me.

It delighted her to shock the young CNAs (certified nursing assistants) by using mild profanity when they came into her room to take care of her daily needs. "Bullshittio on that!" she'd say, when they announced her tardy breakfast was on the way, followed by, "That's a nicer way of saying bullshit, isn't it?"

One of the many reasons I chose to write this book was to inspire you to adopt a forgotten elder in your community. A large dose of humor, especially in an unexciting nursing facility, can make a world of difference to a wheelchair-bound senior. The idea emerged on my first date with Bee at the care center. I had only half an hour to spend with her, so instead of getting together in her room, Bee suggested I meet her in the dining room, saying she wanted to surprise me. Nothing can flabbergast you quite like the antics of an 85-year-old prankster.

Picture this… I'm sitting at one of 20 round tables in the spacious dining room. Early afternoon light filters in from the wall-to-wall windows on one end of the room, and several seniors are already seated in their assigned places. I'm eyeing the doorway expecting Bee to arrive any minute while a few more seniors are wheeled in by their cheery CNAs. Ten minutes go by.

Most of the tables were filled with people waiting for their lunches; two or three at this table, a solo senior at that one. A catchy tune by Frank Sinatra blared out from the overhead speakers, and a pleasant aroma drifted in from the kitchen. Four or five staff members were carrying green plastic trays of food to the waiting seniors. It was strangely quiet; the only voices I heard were the dining room personnel asking who wanted milk, juice or water. Most of the seniors sat silently, staring down at the napkins and metal flatware in front of them. Sometimes it felt more like a prison with strict NO TALKING rules than a nursing home.

Just when decided to go fetch Bee, she appeared, standing at the doorway with her walker. No one looked at her but me. She waited. This was clearly intended to be a shining Miss America moment, and it's evident she wasn't going to blow her entrance. If I hadn't started to shriek uncontrollably, I bet Bee might have stood there all day waiting for someone to notice her. Gradually, a chortle began, then a few snickers, followed by some genuine guffaws from the kitchen staff, cueing Bee to walk slowly into the room. Here she comes, Miss Granny A-mer-ic-a. On the top of her head were shiny pink rabbit ears. Fluffy red and black slippers in the shape of ladybugs were on her feet; three times her size. And, for the pièce de résistance, she was wearing large black glasses with the familiar bulbous nose and bushy eyebrows of Groucho Marx. Just as the chuckling was about to subside, she reached up to the end of the nose and turned a small knob. Groucho's eyebrows and moustache twitched comically, cracking everybody up all over again.

Thankfully, Bee rarely visited the somber island where seriousness is king, preferring to actually live by Rule No. 6, even after enduring a walloping seizure.

> BEE: I got up to turn down the volume on the TV when the phone rang and my pants fell down, so now I'm working to pull them up. I didn't time it right for your call, did I?
>
> KELSEY: No problem, Bee. How are you feeling today?
>
> B: I'm thinkin' that I had another seizure.
>
> K: Yes, you had one yesterday. We talked twice afterward.

B: Was I decent? Oh shit. I didn't make you feel like you did it to me, did I?

K: Of course not.

B: Oh, good. I've been practicing Rule #6 lately.

K: I think you wrote the book on Rule #6, Bee.

B: You won't believe this. I am still alive.

K: I think the first clue was that you answered the phone.

B: Oh, yeah, that's true, isn't it? Here's the funny thing: I brushed my teeth last night.

K: Well, that's great. What's so funny about it?

B: Well, I thought the toothpaste tasted a little different, but I'm dopey at night anyway. I brushed my teeth with the prescription in a tube. It was the anti-itch cream. And you know I felt better this morning? I didn't itch anywhere.

K: You, my beautiful friend, are a hoot!

B: It's unusual, isn't it? I've been thinkin' *you better put this in the book*. I'm laughing my ass off this morning. You know, God handles these things. Nobody woke me up for breakfast, but I still got my favorite cereal. I call it "Smart and Fart." Do you know what it's really called?

K: I think it's called Smart Start, but I promise not to tell Kellogg's you changed the name.

The famous Irish playwright, novelist and poet Oscar Wilde, popularly known for his barbed wit, wrote, "Seriousness is the only refuge of the shallow." Along with her epitaph, "Getting Better" and "I lived by Rule No. 6," Bee told me she wanted to be remembered as someone whose thoughts were deeper than a puddle and how often she made people laugh. I'm certain Wilde, who decorated his college dorm room with peacock feathers, sunflowers and blue china, would have been proud of Bee.

With a penchant for getting right to the point, have you noticed in our dialogues that Bee frequently began her sentences with "I've been thinkin'?" Not think-*ing*, but the short, Southern drawl version – thinkin'. It's a contagious leadoff since I've been thinkin' a lot more myself since we started these spelunking conversations ten years ago. And since we were talking about the benefits of Rule #6, I reflected on the times when I took myself *very* seriously, remembering how I wasn't served at all by taking that tack.

I joined Bee's rebel club the day I walked into her room and showed her the tattoo on the inside of my left wrist. There are two Japanese kanji symbols there now, essentially translated as "humor." I carry these as a reminder of Rule No. 6.

Bee's response when I showed my tattoo to her was to ask when she could get one, too. Hers, she said, would be a giant heart somewhere on her upper chest where everyone could see it to remind them the importance of loving each other.

I don't always know how to do things. That's silly. There's a God way to do it.

7. Is God a He or a She?

"I pray to God a lot. I say, "God, get me to the toilet on time,
and I mean dry and clean."
– Bee Landis

"The help of God is closer than the door."
– Old Gaelic saying

Bee and I have tossed around many diverse subjects in the more than 700 conversations that inspired this book, but none were more prevalent than our discussions about God. That makes perfect sense, of course, since Bee is a minister. But given that Bee has little memory of the Bible or her path to becoming a Science of Mind reverend, it's been fascinating listening to her grappling with the concept of God. In many of our conversations, as persistent as a Seattle rainfall, was the question of whether God is a He or a She. One of the reasons God is translated as a "He" in English is because there are no gender-neutral pronouns in Hebrew, i.e. there is no equivalent of the English "it." But Bee has no memory of that.

There were many lively discussions between us concerning the suggestion that God is perhaps neither a He nor a She but a gender-neutral entity or a transcendental force.

KELSEY: Along with others in the Christian faith, I hear you say all the time, "Thank you, Father." Do think there is a "Mother" God? Is God a He or a She?

BEE: I do find myself saying "He," and yet not wanting to say "He," as if God is a man. A part of God is nature and I see both the masculine and feminine there. One cannot survive without the other. I find myself looking at things happening, and saying, "Okay, that's the feminine of it, or that's the masculine of it. I see God as a "Him", knowing that "She" is there supporting God all the way.

K: What about the part that says we were "made in His image?"

B: I think that's nonsense. The beliefs that have taken me all my life to attain have to be based on an example. And the only example I had was in the Bible. And who wrote that? Man.

K: Some suggest that the male-dominated society in Biblical times artificially imposed and even promoted the image of God as a male human.

B: It's worked, too. But then I find myself thinking, who invented God? God keeps changing sexes, doesn't He? So, listen up and pay attention to what She is saying.

To those devoted ones whose spiritual faith is immutably clear and irrevocably intact, I salute you. At times I feel the agony that the 13th Century Persian poet, Rumi, must have felt when he said, "There is no worse torture than intellectually knowing about Love and The Way."

I have experienced an on-again-off-again passionate relationship with God; a complex stew of ideas, doubts, dreams and beliefs, each morphing into the other, sometimes changing radically from one minute to the next. When Bee innocently shared her thoughts and fears with me about her relationship with God, it serves as a cosmic two-by-four across my forehead, encouraging me to dig — as deeply as she does — inside the womb of my own beliefs.

B: I can't imagine what a connection to God would be, if not on a personal level. When I am talking to God, nobody else is talking to Him. I know that sounds corny.

K: It sounds like you know you have a personal relationship with God. I suspect that is available to anyone who chooses to connect consciously with their Source.

B: There is nothing that can jolt my thinking today. I hear these heavy religionists quoting Jesus, but not living the way Jesus lived. Jesus never wanted to start a war. God doesn't want to start a war. I don't want to start a war.

K: Ah. I wish some of our world leaders thought that way. Many lives would be saved. Suffering would be reduced enormously.

B: Yes. Everything hinges on something, doesn't it?

K: Our fear-based thinking and beliefs, most of all. It all starts with our thoughts and spreads out to our emotions.

B: I think Jesus must have said, "I'm not going to get my hands in this and shake you up. I could save you, but what for? That's your work to do. I'll give you any kind of help you want – all the tools, but it's your job to use them." We are prophets all the time. We have all these thoughts in our heads; sometimes they're positive thoughts but more often than not they are negative. Seems to me it's a good idea to kick out the negative ones and only focus on the positive ones. That's what the old prophets like Jesus did.

K: And Isaiah and Moses and St. Francis and Buddha and Muhammad and Rumi and many others.

B: Yeah, I guess so. I know more about Jesus than those others, but I know he wasn't alone in his "propheting," maybe just the best.

K: What do you think is the truth about Jesus?

B: I think that he was everything he implied he was. I don't think he set himself up to be worshiped at all. I believe he led people to their own "hero-ship."

K: Maybe we are too afraid to find out who we really are underneath the skin. We tend to elevate Jesus to a deity that we believe we can never become.

B: It might make us terribly responsible.

K: And we may not want that responsibility.

B: We fear it.

After we ended that conversation I spent the better part of the day ruminating about what Bee said, and it was both challenging and playful. I wondered if we fear the responsibility of being fully human, or is our fear that we are spiritual beings living human lives and we don't have the faintest clue what that really means. "Ah," I thought, "so that is what Marianne Williamson[8] meant when she said, 'Our deepest fear is not that we are inadequate. Our deepest fear is that we are powerful beyond measure. It is our light, not our darkness that most frightens us.'"

Even the mind of Einstein had a burning desire to know who or what God was. Buckminster Fuller, the famous American visionary, thought of God as a verb rather than a noun.

Halfway through her eighth decade on earth, Bee didn't shy away from expressing her inner fears, even if they revealed some of her darkest torments.

"Sometimes I feel guilty about ignoring God," she mentioned during a particularly revealing conversation, "but then I realized I have ignored 'me' most of my life, too, so what did I expect?"

When I questioned her further, she clarified what she meant.

B: All my life, I think, I've felt guilty and unworthy. I'm not sure about what because my memory is so loose. But the feeling is here today even without any memory. I think if I hadn't ignored what I was feeling back then, I'd be free of those guilty feelings today.

K: So, what you're saying is that it's important to acknowledge what we are feeling all the time? Is that it?

---

[8] http://www.marianne.com/

B: It's vital, otherwise you end up in a place like this, wondering what in the hell your life was all about. The only way I can die better is to live better.

K: Guilt is simply blame turned inward. What are you blaming yourself for now?

B: For believing in a mediocre God – and a mediocre me. I realize it may not be just my problem, but everyone's problem: not seeing God as big enough.

K: Each of us has a unique relationship with our God. Some people don't believe in God, or any deity for that matter, preferring the science of evolution as the explanation for who we are.

B: Ask them if they can make a cockroach.

K: (laughing) There are millions, perhaps billions, of beliefs. That's okay. I think they all work out eventually. I believe we're all climbing the same mountain.

B: I've got a feeling that I'm going to last a few more years and I'm going to look back on this time as the "Great Gelling."

An ongoing fantasy for Bee was to return to some kind of ministry, whether it was to the young CNAs or a small group of fellow seniors. Even if this were a pipe-dream, due to her declining mental dexterity, I admired her determination. Bee pulled fortitude out of her bag of tricks in a way that constantly amazed and surprised me. I wouldn't have rained on her parade for anything in the world.

B: I've been thinkin' about doing a talk on the *Unchurchiest Church*. What do you think about that?

K: I think that's a catchy title.
B: Me too. I keep thinking about what would happen if — and I mean if — Jesus came back.

69

K: A lot of people have thought about that for nearly 2,000 years. The entire Christian religion is based on the promise that Jesus will return to earth.

B: Well, okay. What if that's all a bunch of BS?

K: Interesting thought. I truly don't know. I'm not sure that it really matters. Mark Twain wrote, "If Jesus came back, the Christians would crucify him."

B: I bet he's right. Since Jesus was a Jew back then and if he returned to earth today, what church would he belong to? Whose team would he be on? There are so many to choose from.

K: Over 20,000 Christian affiliations alone. I imagine the Catholics and Protestants wouldn't like it much if Jesus chose to be a Jehovah's Witness or Mormon.

B: Oh, but it would be fun to watch, wouldn't it?

Maybe the whole idea of adopting an elder is to help caregivers look at who we are underneath our suits of clothes. While we are stimulating their questions about God and the afterlife, maybe we are simultaneously revitalizing our *own* faith. Similar to a child who doesn't blink when she says "I don't like you" to a perfect stranger, our elders have nothing to lose by calling it the way they see it. We just have to give them a chance.

Anyone who made it through the technological advances of the past century — from automobiles to lunar landings and from one war to another and another and another — deserves all the respect they can get. I don't know if I'm going to make it to my senior years, but it is anticipated that at least forty million of my fellow boomers will. The question is, how do we want our final chapters to read?

I don't think I'm going out on a limb by saying that I believe one of the big reasons Bee continues to ask all these questions about what her purpose is, and about life and God, is because I *ask* her. And I invite her to ask me right back.

B: How big is your God?

K: Today? Infinite.

B: Do you call him Father?

K: No I don't. The word "father" relates to a human being, but for me, God is an infinite omnipresent energetic mystery.

B: God *is* a mystery. I keep wanting Him to stand up.

K: Go, Bee, go. As you've said, we're both floating on God's energy anyway.

Our daily talks were not designed to determine whether God is female, male or that giant ball of fire-energy we call "the sun." They *were* intended to promote and evoke courageous probing within the inner sanctum of our spiritual consciousness. People all over the world are searching for a deeper, cosmic meaning to their lives. In our often frantic quest for spiritual truth, we tend to forget that the answers reside right here inside our own hearts. The books, the ministers, the rabbis, the seminars and the channeled mystical helpmates from other realms are all here to lend a hand, to offer guideposts, but not necessarily to provide the definitive answer. Maybe there isn't just one answer, but as many as there are people asking the questions.

Years ago I drove to Portland, Oregon to participate in an audience with His Holiness, the Dalai Lama. Surrounding me were more than 4,000 eager devotees, aspirants and the simply curious, waiting for His Holiness to address the gathering. After thanking us for our interest in Buddhism, he bowed respectfully and said, "I want you to know that all your paths work."

Bee agreed completely.

B: Even though I was happy as a Science of Mind minister, today I know I could walk into any church, anywhere, and be happy. I believe we all search for the same thing: to be ONE with God, and to experience it and express it in every avenue of our lives.

A couple of years back we were reading about inner peace in the *Daily Word*. Responding in the gentlest way, she said "I don't believe God either takes away or gives to me inner peace. I believe I bring that to myself. I have a choice."

K: What is that choice?

B: To either succumb to it or say, "The hell with you."

K: So the real power is in you. In us?

B: Yes. But who created it?

K: Great question, Bee. Who, or what, do you think created it?

B: I don't believe there was anything before God. So God is the winner.

K: Maybe we're all potential winners, Bee. I think that was Jesus' purpose, to remind us *God is within* us.

B: Jesus lived by the Christ Force within him and encouraged us to live by the Christ Force within ourselves, too. I wonder when we're going to get that.

For me, reducing abstract concepts — like God or the outer mystical realms — to the simplicity of a single red rose or the soothing sounds of a Native American flute, is comforting. The *Daily Word* topic one day was on The Rhythm of Life. "Oh, I know what that means," Bee said guilelessly. "That's dancing with God."

I don't think that anything that happens to us is permanently implanted. It just passes through.

8. My Death Has Been Delayed

"Death is not the greatest of evils; it is worse
to want to die and not be able to."
– Sophocles

"If I'm going to die, I want to learn to die better."
– Bee Landis

A few months ago I was visiting some old friends who live in the hills high above the ocean in Laguna Beach, California. When I walked through their front door I was greeted by one of their dogs, an old chocolate lab by the name of Cody. With milky eyes, nearly blind from cataracts, he limped over to me, obviously in considerable pain. Small drops of urine dribbled across the tiled floor as he made his way to my feet. Old dogs become incontinent, too. It was shocking to see his skeletal structure protruding under his dull brown coat, and I had to ask my friends, "What part of Cody's message are you not getting?"

My friends adored their dog; there was no question about that. They were responsible, loving people who sought routine veterinary care for him. They just didn't want to let their beloved pet go. Sometimes we ask our pets, *and* our elders, to go on living for *us*, but allowing them to die with dignity – when they're ready – may be just another way of living – formless and free.

Bee has helped me understand that the issue is not about granting longer life to our elders. It's about whether modern medicine can contribute to making old age an honored and dignified time of life, rather than a miserable life sentence.

Anyone who knew Bee would attest, with a hearty laugh, that Bee loved life, even while living in a care center. She loved talking with people, challenging them to look her square in the eyeball if they happened to avert their gaze. The slightest touch on her back would instantly produce purrs and moans of contentment. Rarely when I called did she not giggle when she heard me say "Helloooooooo, Bee." Often, she'd strut right in to whatever she had been reading that day, such as the *Daily Word*, praising the topic, "Let Go... Let God," as if she'd never read it before.

The *Daily Word* was one of the deepest connections between us, and we read it together for nearly ten years. Bee would read the first paragraph, sometimes with difficulty, even with the larger font we ordered for her, and I would read the next. Often we'd be amazed at how the topic was just what we both needed to hear that day. This is in striking contrast to what I have witnessed in the other nursing facilities I've visited over the years. Most of the seniors I've encountered in these places were stuck in that dreaded triangle of loneliness, helplessness and boredom. On any given day I'd see groups of elders sitting in their wheelchairs in the hallways, sleeping or staring wordlessly at nothing in particular. Some would watch television or sleep most of the day, barely interacting with one another, and rarely did any of them ever smile. Bee did not fit that stereotype. She was actually happy most of the time, bucking the norm, defying statistics and creating her own world.

> BEE: I'm enjoying life more; analyzing, thinking that life is getting better even though I feel like I am approaching the end of it. Around the corner of the road I see a possibility that this is just a turning point where I get my thinking straightened out before I die.

> KELSEY: My sense is that all the work we are doing here on earth is preparing us for our death in some way. It's amazing to me how uncomfortable people get around the word "death." We will all get there someday. There's a great saying: "No one gets out of this world alive."

> B: It's approached hardly at all around here.

> K: Not just there in the care center, Bee. In general our American culture rarely wants to talk about death, as if ignoring it will somehow make it magically go away. It would seem to me that if people were encouraged to talk about death, they just might relax a little.

B: The ill spell (seizure) I had this last week made me feel more aware of myself, my body and my health than any other thing that has happened, which kind of scared me into becoming more tranquil. Does that make sense? That may not be the word I want, but its close.

K: I have a theory that all through our lives we are given the chance to let go of things, of ideas, of dreams, of our youth. Perhaps it's a job or a relationship or our health for a period of time, like when someone gets a chance to deal with illness. Each one is an opportunity to learn to let go gracefully, without years of suffering, sniffling or regret. If we learn to do that successfully, when we are faced with what I call the BIG LET GO, the moment we let go of our physical bodies, then graceful acceptance will be as natural as exhaling. *Ahhhhhh.*

B: I don't think this world is fatal.

K: This world may be just a stopping-off place, like a roadside diner. Lots of fun stories come out of roadside diners.

B: Yeah. I don't think that anything that happens to us is permanently implanted. It just passes through.

In the United States we are not permitted to die of "old age." In 1951 The National Office of Vital Statistics ordered all state and federal agencies to adopt a standard list of 130 contributing or underlying causes of death, but the list did not include "natural causes due to advanced age." You will not see "old age" written on a death certificate, but rather an individual, named disorder. Perhaps doctors feel better if they lose the fight with a nasty disease they can easily identify, like Alzheimer's or colon cancer, but they are stymied by the concept of a natural, destined old age that they can't fight or control.

This is not news, but I'm going to say it anyway because most of us seem to be in deep, dark denial about the inevitability of our deaths: You and I *will* die someday. No exceptions.

One of the lovely things about Bee is that she's comfortable talking about death – both hers and mine – most of the time. On some days she's aware and accepting of the natural course of her own human life, though on other days she's not. I remember when I was sitting with her in our favorite sandwich restaurant in Bishop. It was right in the middle of summer and tourists were milling all around us, crowding the restaurant, bumping in to her wheelchair and making her wince.

"Hey there!" she shouted at an unsuspecting vacationer who had inadvertently kicked the big wheels of her chair as he was trying to make his way to the exit door. "I'm in here! Don't you see me?"

And then she looked at me and said, "That's the problem with getting old. You become invisible."

Fear of the unknown ranks right up at the top of the list of almost anyone's List of Terrors, and Bee is no exception. What happens the second after we take our last breath has been the subject of endless debates since we created language. Here's what Bee had to say in her own unique language:

B: Why do we treat death as a shocking thing? We think it's the worst thing that can happen to us, as if we've never done it before.

K: Do you think it's because we don't know what's going to happen?

B: Maybe. We think it's never happened before.

K: What if we had the awareness that death has happened to us hundreds, if not thousands of times before in other incarnations?

B: I don't know. I have never personally talked to anyone who has died.

K: Maybe we're so terrified of death because it's so ordinary. It happens all the time.

B: I wake up and I look at my hand and it's gripping, but I'm not holding on to anything at all. So what do I

think I'm holding on to? My life here? What am I
attached to? I don't know. Maybe I am getting prepared
to die, so I trust God to tell me when it's time.

There's a line I remember reading sometime during the two years
of research for this book that stuck with me. It said that essentially the
knowledge that modern medicine cannot cure everything does not stop
the desire to try. Since modern medicine has thus far found no cure for
old age, then all of us will eventually die of something. So for whom –
or what – is modern medicine doing all this trying? Is it for the frail,
elderly patient or the ongoing science of discovery?

If it's for the patients, then it seems we would want to inform the
patients of what we're up to, i.e. "We're going to try to keep you alive,
mom, no matter what." If science is the motive, then elders and future
elders are not much more than disposable lab animals. There is nothing
more distressing than feeling dependent and useless in one's golden
years, so where's the benefit in keeping a loved one alive, no matter
what? It may be helpful, if you are ever faced with an issue like this
concerning a loved one, to remember that there is a difference between
prolonging life and *prolonging death.*

Every time Bee and I scratched the surface of a long-held belief
and exposed the truth underneath, we literally became giddy with
excitement, as if we were the only people who had ever questioned
utterly useless beliefs. Often, it was an ecstatic experience for both of us,
overflowing with chill thrills. For years I've felt my own version of chill
thrills when a spiritual truth from my heart was rising to the surface.
Think of billions of tiny champagne bubbles washing across your skin
and you'll get the idea. Considering the possibility of reincarnation filled
up nearly an hour of juicy discussion.

K: Do you know what I've noticed, Bee? I've noticed
that Buddhists and Hindus who believe in reincarnation
aren't as afraid of dying as Christians seem to be. Why
do you think that believing in reincarnation seems to
contribute to a more peaceful death?

B: I'm getting over being fearful of dying. I'm getting ready to let go of there being finality to life.

K: Are you getting that your soul life goes on?

B: Yes, but it's not enough for me just to say life goes on forever and ever and ever.

K: So, what do you want now?

B: I don't know.

K: Maybe you do. Look again.

B: I've tried over and over not to face death, I think. How many people my age are excited about this thing called dying? Nobody talks about it around here. I'm finding little surges of courage and...(making a long moaning sound)...*ooooh.*

K: What is that feeling?

B: A chill thrill.

Some of us contemplate the meaning of life ad nauseam, but rarely do we contemplate the meaning of death. I figure that's why we are so reluctant to bring up the subject of death with our elders. Not only do we not want to consider that they are going to die, possibly soon, but many of us don't want to acknowledge our own imminent demise.

Do you remember walking into a dark room when you were a kid, your little fingers groping around on the wall for the errant light switch? Your heart was beating loud enough to hear it down the block, and your mind conjured up every Dracula/Mummy/Wolf-Man monster you'd ever seen, lying in wait for you. But then, all of a sudden your hand finds the switch, turns it on, and voilá! Let there be light. That's what happens when we allow ourselves to start talking about the unthinkable. We illuminate it with truth-clarifying light. No more monsters.

According to some secular Western scholars, most of the world's religions were created because humans were afraid of death. I don't want to get into a religious argument here, but what I do want is to encourage a dialogue between caregivers and elders, and most of all between us and us, connecting our intellects with our hearts in a way that keeps the floodgate open. Caregivers are in a uniquely privileged position to help elders develop peaceful exit strategies, and this is a dialogue that can make a difference between a peaceful death and one that is rife with stress and fear.

After Christianity became the *ex cathedra* religion of the Roman Empire, references to reincarnation in the New Testament were deleted by the emperor Constantine at the Council of Nicaea in the fourth century, and reincarnation was declared heresy.[9] It was officially banished by the Christian Church in the sixth century. Maybe Constantine felt it was threatening the stability of the empire or maybe the church concluded that its flock would be less obedient if they believed they would have another shot at redemption. Forcing the idea of a single Judgment Day for all wields a mighty sword. We've been subjected to the power of forced fear for millennia, and it's about time we take our power back by asking the simple question... *who is thinking for you?*

What if an older patient chooses, with or without having consulted family, to refute care or reject a treatment option offered by her medical team? Would that suggest that the elder lacks decision-making capacity? Hardly. Unlike Cody, the aging dog who could only communicate on a primitive level, most of our elders have the capacity to declare their intentions verbally, but we're just not listening. Reciting tales of miraculous recovery that we've heard from others or via the media, we reassure our elders that they can heal, too, and, by golly, we're gonna fight this thing.

Sometimes those miraculous recoveries do happen, but it's a decision for the *patient* to make, assuming he or she is mentally alert enough to do so. One way we're demonstrating how tightly we cling to life at any cost is to look at the outrageous amount of prescription drugs our elders are taking. By the time most Americans are 80 years old, many of them are taking eight different drugs a day at an *average* cost of

---

[9] *Nicaea: A Book of Correspondences*, Martin Rowe, Lindisfarne Books - 2003

81

$400 a month. Chalk it up as another financial win for the pharmaceutical companies, at the cost of human dignity. In no way am I condemning the need for necessary medications for our elders or anyone else, but often, however, we continue to take medications long after they are required, or long after the drug should have been replaced by changes in lifestyle. And, often the mixture of drugs can be counterproductive, so it is always prudent to become a *full participant* in one's medication program.

Being unable to grasp what the world beyond death will look like was disturbing for Bee, but the opportunity to talk about it trumps the other inane conversations she's inclined to have during a typical day at the care center. Even though the topic may be uncomfortable, it doesn't keep her from looking, asking and digging deeper into her emotional toolbox of unexplored fears, analogous to the possibility of those post-death destinations known as heaven and hell.

B: I have no disagreement with dying. I just don't want to go yet. I want to hang around this earth a few more years. And then I think, *well Bee, nobody wants to die,* but maybe I shouldn't say that. Some people do want to die, but they aren't allowed to go. Their family will be upset. The doctors will keep them alive.

K: Do you think we will ever learn to accept the natural goodness of death?

B: I'm beginning to have more faith in the goodness of death. Although sometimes when I think that death is fairly close, I don't like that much.

K: My deepest heart tells me that death is just one more change; another phenomenon that happens throughout our lives. We keep thinking that physical life is all there is, or that when we die we will go to some mythical heavenly place. What do you think?

B: What I'm happy about is all the positive stuff. I'm not dreaming any frightening nightmares about dying. I'm sure people have horrible dreams. I'm not aware of anything like that happening to me. I have asked it, *are you a dream or are you real?*

K: What if you changed your language to "dream state" and "physical state?" They are both relatively "real."

B: This is all new to me. Although I'm not ready to die yet, I'm not afraid to go to heaven.

K: Do you think there really is a heaven and hell, the way it is described in the Bible? It has been said that religion is for people who believe in hell and spirituality is for those who have already been there. So, what is hell for you?

B: Not being happy.

K: What if the life force that leaves our body when we die starts to leak out early? That's what I would call the walking dead. We're breathing but there is no deep heart connection, no happiness, and very little joy. What if elders who live in care centers like yours have no reason to get up in the morning or live at all, but they're not being allowed to die?

B: I've thought about what would happen if you weren't in my life. Dying is not easy. It's one of the hardest things I've ever done.

K: Tell me more.

B: I'm seeing the other side of things.

K: Like what?

B: I have received a lot of good. I've thought I was getting ready to die. So, I've come to the conclusion that I want to be well or whole. I don't want to be an invalid.

K: Wow! Bee, that's quite a commitment! What I hear is that no matter when you die, you'll be ready.

B: I realize my family doesn't want me. They don't want to be bothered with me. I have a feeling I haven't earned it. And I think they'll feel badly about that. But I don't want that for them. It's their lessons. It isn't a fatality – the end of everything.

K: No, Bee, it isn't. All of life continues in some form. We are such a tiny speck in the Great Mystery. What a breakthrough for you!

B: Oh, yes. I'm rather proud of myself. I didn't realize how important it is to talk with my family. You helped me with that, admitting to myself how important it was. I'd go many days thinking about it, but not wanting to say anything. It's not that I want to suffocate him (her son, Larry), but I want to have a feeling before I die that he was still my son.

Rather than just learning how to live better, maybe it *is* just as important that we learn how to die better. With Bee's help, I'm convinced that living well means accepting and delighting in the inevitable changes in our lives.

The decision to befriend elders in their final stages is sacred territory. It can result in a deep exchange between souls, each seeing the other with joy-filled eyes, and relating to the other with open hearts. It's never too late to embrace these tantalizing stages in a human life – right up to the end. That's why relationships are so critically important to our evolution. Sadly, too many of our elders are being abandoned to experience this ultimate journey alone.

9. Open WIDER

The dying are more alive than ever...
because they realize the futility of fear.
–Father Farrow

"I have an understanding that what I accept intellectually isn't what I
believe at depth. The two need to get married someday."
– Bee Landis

The data are fuzzy when it comes to accurate numbers of America's
elders who are deserted in long-term care centers. Several books on
elders declare it a myth that our parents and grandparents have been
dumped into these facilities, but most studies indicate that as many as a
third of elders in our nation's nursing homes are rarely, if ever, visited
by anyone.

The question is, why? Is it a function of not having enough time?
Are we so overburdened in our daily lives that one more tug on our
coattails is one too many? Do we feel inadequate when faced with a
mentally declining mother who seems to become more of a child every
time we visit her, or a father who doesn't remember our names one day,
or what despicable things he may have done to us when we were 10
years old?

It may be easier to simply walk away from the catastrophic
changes we observe in our aging parents. We might tell ourselves that
our parents are in good hands in a trustworthy facility, or we might
choose to simply not deal with an aging parent who was negligent and
abusive. We may be so wounded that we shut down our hearts
completely.

When I was growing up in the 1950s and 1960s one did not discuss
taboo topics like sex or enigmatic male/female relationship issues.
Religion and politics were only slightly easier subjects around my
family's dinner table, and once uncorked, my sister and I learned quickly
the advantages of being "seen and not heard." A hit television show of
the era, *Father Knows Best,* idealized middle-class family life in a made-

for-Hollywood fantasy where kids were perfectly imperfect and the always-smiling mom wore pearls, high heels and a perfectly ironed dress when she vacuumed the spotless carpet. And of course the trusted father always knew what was, well... *best*.

I don't know what reality the shows' writers and producers lived in, but that TV family was from another planet as far as I was concerned. Secretly, however, I dreamed of having parents as loving and supportive as wise old Jim and convivial Margaret Anderson. None of the viewing public ever knew that Robert Young, the actor who played Jim, was an alcoholic or Laurin Chapin (who played cute little Kathy) developed a nasty heroin addiction in real life. So it goes with delusion. We want to believe what we want to believe.

The reason I bring this up is because although we might *think* we know what goes on behind our neighbors' closed doors, we have no way of knowing the real truth. Life as an adolescent in conservative Orange County, California may have appeared idyllic to an outsider, but the harsh reality behind my front door was horrifically abusive on all levels. We tend to hold on to those negative experiences throughout our adult lives, reeling the painful memories in again and again, conveniently using them to justify our unhealthy behaviors and the problems in our lives. That's like pulling in a long-dead fish at the end of our line expecting it to be edible. The word "putrid" comes to mind, and it perfectly describes what happens to these memories when they are so fiercely clung to. The same counterproductive excuses are used often to justify abandoning our elders to long-term-care institutions.

The relationship Bee had with her son was none of my business. The relationship you have with your elders is also none of my business. "Not my suitcase," as a dear friend often reminds me when the compulsion comes over me to open up other people's symbolic luggage and re-pack it for them.

Having experienced a less-than-optimal childhood with parents who were about as screwed up as any two people could be while still functioning in the real world; I can understand the dispassionate attitude some of my fellow baby-boomers have toward their elders. My mother was president of the PTA when she wasn't out drinking four-martini lunches, and my step-father, president of the local school board, thought it a fun sport to bring out the strap regularly. Perhaps this has a lot to do with why I bonded so intensely with Bee. It was an act of healing for both of us.

In the months preceding my mother's death, Bee helped me open my heart in a way I never thought possible. Without her impassioned guidance and encouragement – often resembling the persona of the kindly crossing-guard at my elementary school – I probably would have allowed my mother to die in a default kind of way. I might have preferred to protect myself rather than risking – and securing – a new relationship with her at her most vulnerable moment.

While Bee is an elder, she was not my mother. My mother, although terminally ill with ovarian cancer for nine months, was only 64 years old when she died. She made her transition at home in her own bed, and was not confined to a wheelchair or tormented by mental illness. Two weeks before she died I climbed into bed with her, literally on my hands and knees, receiving her open arms of compassion when she noticed I'd been crying. At that moment, 38 years (my age at the time) of negative memories, unfulfilled expectations, thwarted intentions and all the other pain I'd been clinging to, simply vanished. We were just two beings holding each other, illumined by our love awash in the soft pink glow from the bedside light.

The first emotionally close, on-going exchange I had with an aging elder in a nursing facility was with Bee. And although we had known each other for 25 years, the brutal baggage I carried from my childhood had no place in our rare relationship. And this was the key to the powerful, life-altering adventure that began on the day I chose to "adopt" Bee.

The idea that someone else, a total stranger, might have a riotously fun time visiting your own mother or father in a nursing home may be of some consolation if you happen to be the adult child of an aging elder. This generous stranger doesn't have the personal history or emotional baggage that you do, and that makes for a clean slate and an open heart.

Back to Bee's spotty relationship with her only son. At first I wasn't aware of any drifting flotsam between the two of them, but it became apparent about three months later when I called Bee only to hear

89

the familiar disconnect tones on the telephone... *"this number is not in service at this time. Please check the number and try again."*

I did dial again, and listened to the same recorded voice droning on. That was the first time the phone was disconnected. After the third time a year later, I realized that her son Larry was responsible for paying all of Bee's bills at the assisted living facility, including the phone bill. He wasn't paying these out of his own pocket, but from Bee's monthly pension and social security checks, which were sent to him for deposit into a joint checking account. Everyone at the care center, from the administrator to the pharmacist to her physician, told me that payments were often months late. How to approach the subject with Bee became my next challenge. It was my intent to discover a solution rather than becoming a stick in the spokes of their relationship.

> KELSEY: This is a bit awkward, Bee, but I'd like you to share your feelings about your son, if it's okay with you. How often do you talk with him?

> BEE: I feel sorry for my son. I know he feels rotten. I want to think about living *and* forgiving. I have to open up my hand and let him discover his own life.

Notice that Bee didn't actually answer my original question about the communication status with her son. The lack of congenial rapport with their adult children is a huge issue for many elders, and this was particularly true for Bee, who had practically no vivid memories of her past. She had no specific images of herself and her son sitting at the dinner table or enjoying a family vacation or a school wrestling match. This could have been a tip-toe moment, but I pressed on anyway.

> K: Will you call your grandsons?

> B: I don't have the phone number.

> K: Yes you do, Bee. Their phone numbers are on a sheet of paper above your bed that says "Larry's Phone Numbers." They are in big red letters.

B: Okay. I'm learning to accept more and say thank you. Sometimes I can't understand why anyone should be loving toward me.

K: I feel very sad to hear that, Bee.

B: Because I feel like I'm a worthwhile person, to be loved openly. But...

K: What's the but, Bee?

B: I don't know. That's what life is all about; figuring out what gets in the way of remembering we are loved. I forgot you put their phone number up there. Thank you for doing that and for loving me.

When we are children our parents can teach us many things, like how to tie our shoes or how to look both ways when we cross the street. But what if those lessons came with a screeching bullhorn delivery and a belt across bare legs? What if our primary education came from the deranged mind and foul mouth of a drunken father? We'd sure learn to hang up our clothes... fast. But what else would we have learned subconsciously? I learned how to run out the back door as my mother was pulling in to the garage.

The dilemma for Bee, and perhaps for other elders suffering from dementia, was that she had a history full of black holes. All she had were clouded shades of reprehensible emotions detached from any specific memory that might allow her to make sense of her family's absence in her life. Akin to many of us who are familiar with carrying a sense of unworthiness throughout our lives, I suspect that Bee probably questioned her true value as well. But she made it perfectly clear to me that she wasn't leaving this world until she'd "learned to die cleaner and better." At the top of her list was having a better connection with the only family she had left

B: Thoughts flash through my head that say, *Now Bee, don't die yet. You can't leave all your unmade papers of work; whatever you haven't finished.*

91

K: How do you know what you haven't done?

B: Well, my son... (hesitating) ...When I talked to him a few days ago I was afraid he was thinking, "Oh, it's her again." But he was so sweet. I had a flash go through my head where he was different than I made him out to be. I want an opportunity for him to know that I love him. I have looked at things between us and thought, *well Bee, why don't you admit it? You won't let Larry be anything other than an unloving son.*

K: Maybe it's time to let that go. What do you think?

B: I think it's long overdue.

As the months went by I didn't notice much of a change in the status with Bee's relationship with Larry. Periodically, on special occasions such as Thanksgiving, her family would drop by the care center on their way to Southern California for a few hours. Those days were pure magic for Bee, who was transformed into a six-year-old while regaling me with every last juicy detail of the visit, including details about their shopping spree at K-Mart or how crisp the bacon was at the local diner. I'd hear the same stories retold again and again for days afterward. "Oh," she'd repeat, "Did I tell you what Larry said to me? He said he's so proud of me. And I just knew he meant it. I think we're really getting close now."

But soon the phone connection between them would fall silent again and weeks would go by with little or no contact while Bee struggled to hold onto a fading memory of their last time together. It broke my heart. But contrary to what I would have expected, Bee never blamed her son for anything, preferring to pile all of the responsibility onto her own shoulders. Throughout our conversations during her first year in the care center, Bee would unexpectedly interject Larry into our conversations, as if he were a permanent squatter in her mind:

B: Maybe I haven't given Larry an opportunity to be close. I didn't think I was of any importance to him, but I haven't listened with an open heart.

K: Why do you think that is?

B: It doesn't matter why. I'm not so wrapped up in the "whys" anymore.

K: What would you need to do to open your heart?

B: Knowing that I want to feel comfortable around him. And I do. It's a matter of feeling, isn't it? When I call him I think he's relieved.

K: That must be a relief and comforting to you, too.

B: Yes. I'm starting to call more often. I thought it was his responsibility to call me. That's bullshit. That's ridiculous.

K: When we love someone, it's all about giving the love, not about what we're hoping to get in return. Is that what you're saying? Whatever we want from someone else, we need to give it first?

B: Exactly. I will feel free when I give myself permission to release my son to his highest good. He wasn't put on this earth to serve me. I never thought about wanting him to be minding me. I want to bawl. I have never wanted to cry.

K: I've never seen you cry, Bee.

B: I know. Getting close to you is what has saved me. There is no accident that you are in my life.

K: You know what, Bee?

B: What?

K: I love you up to the sky and the moon.

B: That far, huh?

It never occurred to me that I might be hurting Bee's son when I sat down with her to discuss my having Power of Attorney in her affairs. She needed a responsible, consistent advocate, and I was more than willing to meet that need, because for whatever reason, Larry was not. What did occur to me, as the old maxim goes, was that blood *is* thicker than water. I suspected that sometime in the future Larry and I would sit eyeball-to-eyeball with each other, hopefully not over Bee's draped coffin, and have a discussion about the last years of his mother's life.

10. Master Bayshun

"The good thing about masturbation
is that you don't have to get dressed up for it."
– Truman Capote

"No matter how old you get, you are still interested
in attracting the opposite sex."
– Bee Landis

Sex was the last thing on my mind when I punched in Bee's phone number in early August, 2005. The hot summer sun was already starting to bake the grassy area outside my office and it was not yet 9:00 in the morning when I settled myself in front of my computer, put on my headset, grabbed my copy of the *Daily Word* and waited for her to answer the phone. The *Daily Word* theme for that day was "Inner Peace," so I was prepared to saunter into a tranquil and soothing chat with Bee that involved deep breathing and visions of colorful meadows of gently waving wildflowers.

Without saying so much as a hello, Bee, as nonchalantly as a TV anchorwoman, announced that she had attended a meeting the day before where the topic was *Sex and Intimacy in Nursing Homes*. I choked as if a rubber band had become lodged in my throat.

KELSEY: What was the topic again?

BEE: You heard me... (reading from the pamphlet) "Define the following: Sexuality. Intimacy. Are you comfortable talking with your co-workers and associates? When is a person too old to be intimate with another person?" Well, hell. Good gravy. I don't even know what intimacy means.

K: Keep going.

B: (continuing to read)... "Should a resident of long-term care facilities be having relationships with other residents?" I guess that means they're screwin' around, huh? (reading on...) "According to AARP, 50% of people over the age of 65 still have sex each week." Well that's something. And there's a cartoon here, too. It shows a man holding a book and there's this thought balloon over his head that says he's wondering whether he should send the book to his mother.

K: What's the title of the book?

B: "Hot Bods over 70."

It's important to remember that Bee had very little long term memory, including the ins and outs of sexual intimacy, no pun intended. It's a subject I hadn't remotely considered she and I would dissect someday. Who or what is God, certainly. What religion would Jesus be if he returned to earth, absolutely. We scrutinized the many angles of death on a weekly basis. Nothing prepared me for "Hot Bods over 70."

Like many, I had fallen into the mindset that stereotyped elders as becoming asexual when they reached their 70s and 80s. Obviously a little research was needed to demystify these myths and misconceptions. What I found changed my perspective completely on the remarkable possibilities of sexual intimacy for elders, or at least what transpires between their *ears*. I'd never look at little old grandmas or grandpas the same way again. Just because they have thinning gray hair, use a walker and forget to put their teeth in occasionally doesn't mean they forget what getting a little nookie might feel like now and then.

One of the few Internet sources I found on sexuality and aging is *Suzi's Loveseat*.[10] This site has been around for more than a decade, and states that its mission is "to rewrite the rules of getting older and transform the voice of aging from one of limitation to one of possibility."

The creators of that site would have done well to have had Bee on its board of directors. Like the wicked rebel she was, she sure as hell

---

[10] www.thirdage.com/loveseat

would have shaken things up, as she did with this totally unexpected revelation in October 2005:

> B: I was willing you to call today.
>
> K: Your will is my command, my friend. What's up?
>
> B: I don't know if I have the courage to tell you, but if I don't then I don't have anything.
>
> K: Go ahead, Bee. You can tell me whatever you'd like. It's all OKAY.
>
> B: Well... (long pause)...I've been thinkin'... (even longer pause)...I've been thinkin'...*about masturbation*. That doesn't shock you or throw you into hysterics, does it?

At this point all I can do is stick my fist in my mouth to keep from laughing out loud – not *at* Bee, but at the exquisiteness of her confession.

> B: I thought that maybe that is what is holding me from my healing; that I need to do it.
>
> K: Wow, Bee! I'm sort of speechless here. Don't get me wrong. I think this is great! Tell me more...uh...what are you thinking exactly about masturbation?

Did I really want to know the answer to that question? I knew that eventually she and I would have to decipher the pronoun "it" that she was so delicately using to describe what she was actually doing or hoping to accomplish, but I needed to stall for some time while I figured out which direction to take.

> B: (laughing) That's the problem... I don't remember. I've never done it that I am aware of. But I have the *overtures* of it. Where I feel like, oh jeepers, something is going to happen but it never does.

99

K: And you have some privacy now that your roommate is gone and you are alone in your room. That should help.

B: But, I couldn't do it.

K: Because you didn't know how?

B: I'm not sure how you do it, but I have the overtures, okay? I've never accomplished it; a feeling of culmination. I think I was always ashamed of it.

K: The culmination you're talking about is called an orgasm. Let me look it up in the online dictionary so I can tell you exactly what it means. *The American Heritage Dictionary* defines orgasm as "the peak of sexual excitement, characterized by strong feelings of pleasure and by a series of involuntary contractions of the muscles of the genitals, usually accompanied by the ejaculation of semen by the male. Also called a climax." I'm honored that you trust me enough to share this.

B: I don't know about the terminology, but I know that I'm awfully red down there. Nearly 85 years old and I'm just learning how to screw around, for crying out loud.

K: It's never too late Bee. It's so amazing that you're allowing yourself to explore this part of your body and your life, especially at your age. It's very brave, and kind of sweet, actually.

B: I ask myself, "Is this why I like men?" Because there is no way that I would have a man today, but I must have some desire there. I gave myself permission to be totally with it and couldn't come up with it. I couldn't have that feeling.

At this point my head felt like it was ricocheting in a pinball machine. A thousand thoughts at once flooded the neuro-streams inside my mind, threatening to send out major TILT warnings. Do I tell her how to have an orgasm? If so, how much detail do I give? Am I willing to share details of my own sex life with her?

Instead of answering these questions, I did a nimble soft-shoe-stage-left instead. What came out of my mouth was this little piece Islamic mystical history, thinking there might be another way for her to participate in the climactic experience that she so obviously wanted.

> K: There are people who practice Sufism who call themselves Whirling Dervishes who offer themselves to God through twirling for hours, even days. They say that they enter into a state of bliss, even experiencing an orgasm that way.

> B: I hadn't thought about bringing God into this.

> K: Hey, darlin', I've got an idea! How about I find some material that you can understand and use that will help you out with this; that will maybe help you to relax a little? The ability to relax is fairly critical to enjoying a successful orgasm for both men and women. Do you think that would help?

> B: Anything at this point will help. I'd ask God, but I think He'd laugh.

There are almost 2 million websites devoted to healthy sex on the Internet, but if you go there to inquire about anything you'll end up with an inbox full of spam promoting pornography, penis enlargement and Viagra. My focus was on finding age-appropriate information for a granny in a nursing facility, and after sifting through get-right-down-to-it titles such as "Intimate Kisses," "Passionate Hearts" and "Private Thoughts," I finally discovered a short masturbation primer on the *Suzi's Loveseat* website. Eureka! Ironically, this easy, step-by-step guide to skillful masturbation was written by a man, something I definitely didn't need to share with Bee.

Given that masturbation is the first sexual act experienced by most males and females, and that 89% of females report they have masturbated[11], it came as no surprise to find over 28 million sites devoted to this pleasurable activity.

I wasn't about to tread through all of them, so I decided that this guy's semi-qualified how-to version would have to do. I printed it out and sent it to Bee inside a greeting card with a photo on the cover of a cuddly pussycat, it's black-and-white whiskered face in an ear-to-ear, tooth-filled grin, hoping she'd get the metaphor. I also prayed that no one at the care center would open it by mistake.

Knowing it would take several days for the masturbation manual to arrive in Bee's expectant hands, I decided in the interim to find as much data as I could on the Internet that might be helpful.

In their 1988 study, Clinical Geropsychologists Bretschneider and McCoy found that 70% of men and 50% of women living in institutional settings had frequent thoughts of wanting a close or intimate relationship with the opposite sex[12]. It was mildly comforting to think that Bee wasn't the only one at the care center with a newly discovered libido.

Bee often confirmed that she regularly had a desire to connect with men more than women, feeling that men looked at her differently or that they would have deeper conversations. Later I would find out from the staff that her interactions with the male population in the care center were not limited to the elder male patient population, but included younger male patients and the young male CNAs who worked there. I doubt that age made any real difference to Bee. She was simply responding to the natural stimulation that occurs when any heterosexual male and female interact, like that arc that occurs when you plug something into a light socket.

At the American Geriatrics Society's 2007 annual scientific meeting, a fascinating study was presented to a group of healthcare professionals. The news that most of these professionals lacked training in elder sexuality wasn't surprising to me and I did not find it particularly comforting either. The study said, "Though nearly 60% of the professionals participating in the study had more than 10 years of

[11] WebMD Medical Reference provided in collaboration with the Cleveland Clinic
[12] Bretschneider, J.D. and McCoy, N.L. 1988 *Sexual interest and behavior in healthy 80-102 year-olds*. Archives of Sexual Behavior, 17, 109-129

experience working with older adults, 70% reported getting no formal training in elder sexuality."

Even though another study by Clinical Nurse Marie J. Kaas was conducted 30 years ago, I would suspect that it still holds true today. She found that "61% of (nursing facility) residents did not feel sexually attractive."[13]

Now there's a piece of gloomy news. If we didn't feel sexually attractive in our 40s and 50s why wouldn't we feel the same way in our 70s and 80s? And what happens to those dismal statistics if we *never* felt sexually attractive? Bee addressed this in a conversation later:

> B: I have felt soiled because I think about sex a lot. When men look at me I see them looking at me and I start to feel guilty. I think God has done me a great favor by making me deal with this.
>
> K: It's beautiful that you're allowing yourself to think and feel all of these things.
>
> B: The only thing I know is that I want to stop feeling bad and guilty about everything. It's not too easy to deal with as a minister. And, to tell you the truth, right now I'm not too interested in being a minister anymore.

When I reminded Bee that she was also a beautiful, magnificent human woman and not just a minister, her reply ripped a bite-sized hole in my heart.

"I have a hard time with that," she quietly admitted. "All I feel is ugly most of the time."

I've always loathed and rarely used that word – *ugly*. It's one of those words that sounds like what it means, especially since it's rarely used in a kind and compassionate way, as *cuckoo* might. Hearing Bee admit she felt ugly most of the time was almost more than I could bear.

---

[12] www.medicalnewstoday.com/articles/69339.php
[13] Merrie J. Kaas, RN, MSN, Sexual Expression in the nursing home, 1978

How do you encourage a woman in her mid 80s to follow directions that prompt her *"to gently rub your flat palms across your chest, above your breasts and then bring them down a little and stroke the sides of your breasts"* when her withered, 80 year-old double D-sized breasts lay flat as a depressed air mattress on her chest? How does she lie back and enjoy *"the sensation your pinched nipples feel when you tease them,"* if she can't find them? How do you convince this courageous elder that she is bringing joy into the world by this loving, self-pleasuring act when she feels just plain ugly and unworthy most of the time?

It was not only Bee's mission to find the answers to these questions, but I was honored to make it my mission as well.

As soon as we hung up the phone that day I decided to take myself and my dogs for a walk in the woods near my house. These frequent walks in the clarity of nature, through the towering ponderosa and fragrant juniper, tiptoeing around golden yellow rabbit brush and purple lupine, would always return me to the simplicity of beauty. It wasn't the perfectly straight ponderosa that caught my eye that morning, but the one that was crookedly gnarled by years of battering wind. It zigzagged to the left and then to the right, so strong was its desire to survive. Are mountaineers not rapturously awestruck by the seeming imperfections and precipitous peaks of the towering Himalayan Mountain, K2? It is by no account considered to be a perfectly structured mountain, but it is formidably beautiful, and that is enough.

A distant and painful sexual memory crept into my mind while on my walk. The sound of my stepfather's feet coming down the hall toward my bedroom stopped my breathing until I was sure he wasn't going to open my door and, like so many other nights, come in and force himself upon me. It was when I heard the doorknob turn that I instinctively crossed my legs and pretended to be asleep.

"You're such a pretty little girl," my stepfather whispered as he lifted my nightgown up to my waist, his large, sweaty hands sliding slowly up my thighs to that private area he knew so well, yet had no right to know.

"Such a pretty little girl," he said again as he tried to pry my crossed legs apart with his fingers.

After he was done I could hear those words echoing over and over again. I always wondered if he would have stolen into my bedroom if he thought I was ugly.

Bee wasn't aware of how her words cut into the depths of my painful memories, but I am grateful to look again, to embrace the opportunity to sweep clean whatever negativity remains. Perhaps on a soul level that is precisely the plan between us, because Bee can't remember her experiences as a child or what encounters may have created her "ugly" belief in the first place. My internal spelunking somehow helped us both.

Maybe the ancient phrase would do well to state "*pretty* is in the eye of the beholder." Pretty connotes something physical, as seen through the eyes. Beauty, as I have come to appreciate the word, implies a *deeper* essence; that which can only be seen beyond the five senses, in the *soul*, as St. Augustine wrote, which only connects through the heart.

For the next several days while I was waiting for the masturbation handbook to get to Bee, our conversations centered on what being beautiful meant. I used this opportunity to encourage Bee to see herself as a being of beautiful light and wonder, to hopefully help her see herself as I saw her.

> K: Long ago I learned that at any given moment we are precisely where we need to be to awaken to our deepest potential. There is no reason to wait. What are we waiting for, anyway? We don't need to be rich or thin or pretty, or have the perfect mate or the perfect job before we can feel the love that is all around us.

> B: That is beautiful, Kelsey. Help me remember this every day, okay? I'm going through a strange time in my life. There's no getting around it. Basically speaking, I'm in a good place because I feel like you don't have to straighten me out every day.

> K: Ah, Bee. I don't think I straighten you out as much as you straighten me out. I get to learn more about who I am through our wonderful relationship.

105

B: Yeah, I feel better too. I feel more capable.

K: That's why relationship is so critically important to human beings. We can mirror to each other who we are and who we aren't, and grow from that experience if we are willing.

B: Sometimes I find that it is not easy to accept this change that is happening, but it's getting easier all the time.

K: Do you feel how beautiful you are, Bee?

B: More and more all the time.

For ten years Bee and I enjoyed our morning phone conversations, which mostly took place at around 9 - 9:30 a.m. Most of my friends and family respected this, knowing that it was not a good time to reach me. While it was rare for Bee to initiate these calls, she had been known to call in the middle of the night, unaware of the time, which was a habit that didn't exactly thrill me. On one such occasion her voice was that of a breathless teenage cheerleader in the final seconds of a winning football game, waking me out of a deep sleep.

B: I am so excited! Your card and the instructions from Master Bayshun arrived today and I've read it and practiced and waited all day to have some privacy and now it's dark and here I am and I knew you would want to know... I just had a WHAMA-LAMA!

11. Exit Strategy
Part Two

"I'm beginning to have more faith
in the goodness of death."
– *Bee Landis*

"So," Bee asked me one day, with eyes as wide and blue as a Montana sky, "what's *your* exit strategy?" It had been months since we discussed her visions of transition.

I'd been so excited over the past few months about working with her precise plans for those final moments in her life that it hadn't occurred to me that I'd been procrastinating creating my own exit strategy. I was within seconds of starting the 650-mile trip back up to Oregon, so I promised her that I'd use the 11 hours of highway driving time to think about her question and I would let her know the answer when I got home.

There are exquisite but desolate stretches of highway between Bishop, California and Sisters, Oregon where I could often drive for more than an hour without seeing another car. Counting golden eagles and red-tailed hawks perched on top of the telephone poles along the road as they looked for prey was always a highlight of my trip home. But this time it was all I could do to manage the speed in which my thoughts raced through my mind. What *about* my exit strategy?

These racing thoughts took me back to the mid-1960s when I was just entering high school, full of myself up to my mascara-ed eyes. The idea of death, specifically *my* death, was as far away from reality as a butterfly is to a hairy caterpillar fattening himself on a green leaf, until a biology teacher taught me to think outside the box. Old Mr. What's-his-name encouraged his students to imagine the inconceivable by asking, "If biology is the science of life, then what is the *opposite* of life?"

The question was germane because we'd been exploring the effects of aging on fruit flies that were subjected to different environments. Looking back, I can see how this applies brilliantly to elders who experience the aging process in nursing facilities around the country.

The average Mexican fruit fly only lives eight or nine days, so the class was able to observe the entire journey from birth to death quite easily. Although we were studying fruit flies and not humans, our teacher was wise enough to give the question a human face.

It was the first time I'd contemplated the idea that I would die someday, but the thought didn't last very long, probably as much a reflection of the culture in which I lived as it was my young age and short attention span. Eastern cultures not only accept death as a natural part of life but spend most of their lives in deep contemplation, even as children, through meditation and other practices that facilitate a peaceful exit from this life, through the dying process and beyond.

But this is not the case in America. I don't remember ever talking with my parents or teachers about death. I only remember hearing what was proselytized from the church pulpit about the glories of heaven and the gruesome bowels of a fiery, ghoulish hell. It was enough to make me not want to die at all, because even though I was a child, I was convinced that I was a sinner. The idea of sin and hell was the closest thing I had to understanding a cause-and-effect relationship between how a soul lives on earth and where it went after death. Even the priests and ministers didn't talk about the death process, so it was not surprising that I spent the first half of my life on earth being completely out of tune with the reality of death. Death is so final and so incomprehensible to the average Western human mind that most of us aren't able to entertain the idea of our own deaths unless forced to through illness or tragedy. This is why, in our modern American culture, so many people suffer emotionally and spiritually during the days prior to their deaths.

Other cultures can teach us valuable lessons about how to prepare for death. It is one of the basic tenets of both Buddhism and Hinduism to believe in reincarnation; both stress living a life of *good karma*, meaning good work or actions.[14] One's life is equally important on day one as it is on the final day; they are inextricably connected. It would be interesting to ponder what really changed the early Christian doctrine that supported the belief in reincarnation until the bishops at the Council of Nicaea modified an existing creed to fit their personal doctrines.

---

[14] Reincarnation: The Missing Link in Christianity, Elizabeth Clare Prophet

Again, I will stress that my observation has been that we do not die any differently than we live. If we want the end of our lives to be peaceful and free from suffering, we would do wisely to live that way now.

Physician-assisted suicide is a reasonable option for many terminally ill patients, and in 1997 the "Death with Dignity" Act was initiated in Oregon, where I live. It allows a terminally ill person to end his or her life through the self-administration of lethal medications expressly prescribed by a physician for that purpose. But what about the hundreds of thousands of elders in nursing homes around the country who are not terminally ill, but *living terminally* without visitors or family?

This is why discussing an exit strategy is so important for both the elder and the caregiver. Opening a dialog about how and where one hopes to die, whether one wants a burial or a cremation, and even the details of the memorial service can prevent needless suffering and confusion for the entire family. (I highly recommend The Five Wishes[15] document as it helps people express how they want to be treated if they become seriously ill and are unable to speak for themselves. Call it a unique living will that covers a broad spectrum of someone's needs: medical, personal, emotional and spiritual.) Creating one's exit strategy is even more specific, a unique image of what you want to see at the moment of your passing.

On that fateful trip home I started thinking about a male patient I once worked with. He wasn't actually lonely, but very near the end of his life he was given an opportunity to create an exit strategy and, when he did, he created a miracle.

During a hospice visit in an impressive San Diego facility several years ago, I heard a piercing alarm go off from behind the closed door of a room just down the hall. Even from twenty feet away I could smell the familiar aroma of marijuana when the nurses opened the door. It turned out that the patient behind that door, "Bob," was a 75-year-old former biker with advanced stage cancer, and that a bunch of Bob's biker-

---

[15] www.agingwithdignity.org

buddies had decided to pay him a visit that day to share some of their favorite pain-killing weed.

Bob had been in palliative care for more than a month, and his adult children were concerned that he was struggling with letting go. I asked them if their father had been visited by a chaplain yet, and they assured me that he most certainly had not, because he was an atheist. But they said it would be okay if I went in for a short chat, issuing a strong caveat that I was not to mention anything about God.

The first thing I saw was a shiny "chopped" motorcycle sitting in the middle of the room. This is not what one normally finds in a hospice room, which is one of the reasons this place was such an impressive facility.

"This is what is called a hog, I believe," I said, admiring the brilliant of orange-flamed artwork on the gas tank and fenders. "I assume this is yours? Very impressive sir. Especially since it's sitting here in your room like a priceless piece of art."

Lying beneath sheets that smelled ever-so-faintly of pot was a sunken-eyed man in obvious pain. Bob and I looked at each other for a moment, silently. It was not necessary to tell him I was a chaplain, because obviously he knew.

"I don't believe in any of that God shit!" he blurted out, the veins on his temples looking like they might rupture.

"That's OK with me," I acknowledged. "What *do* you believe in?"

For a minute or so he just looked away as if he would find the answer in another part of the room. With one excruciatingly thin, pale hand he pointed toward the motorcycle.

"I believe in *that.*"

Moving a little closer to the bed, I smiled. "Tell me some stories about you and your motorcycle, Bob. Tell me where you've been and what y'all did together that put a smile on your face."

It didn't take him long to float back in time as he reminisced about a special Grand Canyon trip he took with his buddies and another cherished story that involved drugs, fast women and fast bikes in the deserts of Nevada. That was back in the days when helmets weren't required, when one could ride on long stretches of open highway without speed limits, when Bob's hair was down to the middle of his back and blew wildly in the wind, all cares and worries obliterated.

It seemed clear to me, as clear as the smile that spread across his lips when he began sharing these psychedelic memories, that these stories were what connected him to meaning in his life. When his smile faded into an expression of sadness and misery, I seized the opportunity to invite him to make his exit strategy right there and then, and it involved his beloved motorcycle.

"You know," I said, "when you're ready to move on, you can get on that motorcycle over there and go anywhere you want, for as long as you want, as far as you want."

By this time I was standing right next to him, my hand lingering on his frail shoulder. "Can you see that as a possibility? Can you close your eyes and see that right now?"

Bob took a deep breath and looked over at his bike, and then slowly closed his eyes. "If only it were that easy," he murmured his voice barely above a whisper.

"It *is* easy if you say it is, Bob. That's your exit. You can make it exactly the way you want."

And Bob did. His family told me he passed away a short time later.

Exit strategies don't require a belief in God or a higher power, as evidenced by Bob's courageous, atheistic heart. All Bob believed in was that motorcycle, which ended up taking him on the final, glorious ride of his life, and just because he said so.

Not long after Bob's death I shared his story with a friend who'd just lost her 75 year-old mother. My friend, in turn, delighted me with her mother's version of a successful exit strategy.

"Mom told me after she retired that she was going to live full-out until the end, and then be hit by a bus," said my friend, oddly laughing. "Even though I thought this was a bit strange, I knew my mother had extremely powerful intent, so I didn't doubt her plan at all."

The previous year my friend's mother had taken a cruise to Indonesia with a couple of old friends. They'd spent the whole day cavorting around Burma as carefree tourists, eating fish cooked in banana leaves and thoroughly enjoying their holiday in the sultry tropics.

When they got back to the ship, my friend's mother was feeling "a little under the weather," so she begged off the evening's activities and went to lie down in her stateroom. Five minutes later she had a massive heart attack. Unfortunately, she had forgotten to bring her advanced directive, which stipulated no resuscitation, but so strong was her intent that even after she was revived and taken to a Burmese hospital, she suffered another and, thankfully fatal, heart attack. It was her version of being hit by a bus.

At the end of my long drive home, the welcome sight of the Three Sisters peaks in the Cascade mountain range signaled I was on the homestretch. I'd been thinking non-stop about the various departures of people I'd known or heard about through my work in hospice, but now all I could hear was Bee's kind but insistent voice echoing inside my head, urging me to answer the question she'd asked 11 hours earlier.

"That's all well and good to think about those other people, Kelsey, but what about *your* exit strategy?"

As I said earlier, I believe we do not die any differently than we live. I've seen it proven over and over again by my loved ones and countless hospice patients with whom I've worked. As a result it has become my daily practice to live as if I were going to die the next day, because living a happy, joy-filled life is as important as breathing. Offering kind, humorous and compassionate self-hugs when I'm in the throes of angst, fearfulness and judgment is also a part of my practice. Accepting total self-responsibility and gratitude for all of it—who I am, where I am, what I'm doing and what I have and don't have—is a powerful bridge that leads to the moment of my death.

And what will that look like? It will look less like any form at all but rather it will have an *essence*, one that is as aware as the sky and peaceful as a mountain meadow filled with thousands of purple lupine.

Although I've only seen a vision of myself once as an old woman (in a dream long ago), I have no objection to being a crone, withered face, body and all. Maybe being hit by a bus or a bolt of lightning isn't such a bad idea after all, but in *my* exit strategy I will *see* the bus coming, instantly realize that I can't get out of the way, and open my arms up in a wide, grateful embrace that simply says, "I'm ready."

114

12. Whom Do You Trust?

"I'm not upset that you lied to me, I'm upset that from now
on I can't believe in you."
– Friederich Nietzsche

Just prior to Thanksgiving, 2006, I attended an annual spiritual retreat at the Serra Center, a Franciscan monastery in the low-lying mountains above the sunny beaches of Malibu, California. It was the first time in nearly a year that Bee and I didn't get to hear each other's voices every day, and I missed her more than I was willing to admit.

Thinking I could connect with her energetically, I went on several solitary beach walks where I collected the most exquisite flat stones with smooth surfaces finely polished by millions of relentless, roiling waves. I thought they might make good gifts for Bee, something I could bring back to let her know I was thinking about her.

For the first several mornings during the retreat I experienced a classic withdrawal/abstinence response, similar to what a drug addict feels after being deprived of a fix, and I realized that I needed a "Bee fix." But cell phones were discouraged at the retreat, so before I left I asked my older sister Barbara if she would be willing to make the daily calls for me, hoping that would be as comforting to me as it was to Bee.

Loyal sibling that she is, Barbara *did* make those calls to Bee, replicating my routine as best as she could, right down to reading the *Daily Word* together, though Barbara had to remind Bee who she was during every call. While I was away Bee had weathered four colossal seizures, two within three hours of each other, one at midnight and the next at three a.m. Barbara reported to me that Bee was frequently confused while I was gone, and this was confirmed when I drove back through Bishop on my way home from the retreat.

Although I'd called Bee twice that morning to let her know I'd be arriving around noon to take her to lunch, I found her asleep in her pink floral nightgown, with the side rails still up on her bed. I'm not sure if she even recognized me when I asked her why she wasn't dressed and ready to go to lunch.

"They won't let me," she said groggily. Her eyes wandered around a bit as if they were trying to get focused.

"Nonsense," I said with all the grace of a marine drill sergeant. I proceeded to get her up, showered, dressed and into her wheelchair in 30 minutes. I was hungry, and all I could think about was the bakery on Main Street in Bishop where our favorite sandwiches were waiting to be made for us.

I rolled Bee into the busy dining area and situated her at a table while I went into the deli to get our sandwiches. Over our heads hung dozens of red, yellow and blue Dutch wooden shoes, representing the Danish background of the locally famous bakery/deli. When I returned, Bee was fully engaged with an eight-month-old baby who was sitting with his young parents at an adjacent table. Both Bee and the little boy were watching the ceiling fan spinning above their heads, its air currents gently knocking the colorful wooden shoes into each other. At one point the baby reached his tiny hand out to Bee, and she responded with the gentlest touch of her fingertips to his. It was as if Bee and the baby were telepathically communicating with each other, their eyes locked in a powerful, unspoken conversation. The baby's father mentioned that his young son had always been delighted by twirling ceiling fans.

"Me, too," Bee said, her eyes moving around like a carousel, perfectly mimicking the baby's eyes.

Bee was so preoccupied with this enchanting baby that she ignored everything and everyone else around her, including her prized turkey sandwich. I was having so much fun watching her watching the baby, that I wouldn't have interrupted their exchange for anything in the world.

Eventually, the couple packed up their son and left the bakery, allowing Bee to whisper with a big smile as she picked up her sandwich, "I so love children," she said, with a long, satisfying sigh. "They remind me of everything that is new and improved."

What a perfect time to offer her the beach stones I'd found during my retreat. I asked her to pick the one that pleased her most. After carefully examining each of the four flat rocks, she chose the one that was my favorite, too. It was a chocolate-colored beauty with a white curling pattern in the middle resembling a universal symbol of gratitude.[16] It fit perfectly in her closed hand, and she held it tightly the rest of the afternoon, stopping every once in a while to look at it and hold its coolness against her cheek.

We sat in relative silence for a few minutes when she looked long and hard into my eyes.

"How long do I get to keep you today?"

"Oh," I replied. "I don't know. Our washer is on the fritz in Mammoth, so I have about six loads of laundry to do at the Laundromat up there."

"Oh, I'd love to help," she offered, meaning it.

"Well," I pondered, "We could find a Laundromat here in Bishop just as well, I bet. How about that?"

"Goody!" she exclaimed.

When we arrived at the Laundromat I wheeled Bee in, making sure her wheelchair was secure and then brought in the laundry from the back of my truck. As I set down the last of the clothes, I noticed her looking with inquisitive eyes at the gift pebble I'd given her. I bent down to get face-to-face with her because there was a particular vision I wanted to share that I felt during my retreat.

"Every time you find yourself a bit out of sorts," I said softly, "you can hold this stone in your hand and envision yourself on a long stretch of beautiful white sandy beach. The blue ocean is next to you, and a perfect mixture of cool and warm air caressing your face. Your bare toes sink softly in the wet sand as the cool water caresses your feet. You can hear the seagulls singing to each other while you breathe in the fresh, salty air. That is this pebble's gift to you."

"Ooh, that's nice," she responded, her eyes still closed, deep in her own imagination.

At some point, after the clothes were whirling around in the machines, she whispered to me, "I'm trying to tell my bowels to be patient."

"Are you saying you have to have a bowel movement, Bee?"

Lowering her eyes a bit, she acknowledged she did.

---

[16] GoGratitude symbol, www.theabundancesite.com

"Well, then, let's get you to the bathroom."

Since Bee wore an adult incontinence pad most of the time, I realized she needed some help getting her pants and the pad down. And because the toilet in the Laundromat bathroom was substantially lower than what she was used to in the care center, when I tried to lower her down slowly, instead she went down with a loud *THUNK* on the hard toilet seat, making both of us laugh.

"Are you okay?" I asked.

She nodded that she was, and wanting to give her some privacy I left assuring her that I would stand just outside the door to help her when she was finished. Several minutes later I knocked softly, asking if she was through.

Her voice was barely audible through the thick door. "I don't know," she said.

I don't know? How can she not know? To find out, I opened the door a little but she was still sitting on the toilet seat, staring up at me quizzically, as if she were waiting for a bus.

"You don't know?" I asked.

"No," she said quietly, staring at the tile floor. "Are you willing to look?"

For a split second I could feel myself hesitate, listening to a range of thoughts flying through my mind. Did I really want to look?

"Sure," I answered quickly, hoping I could sneak a peak between her legs and see whatever was in there. No luck. It was just dark.

"Well, I think we're going to have to get you up, Bee," I said, while reaching under her arms to lift her up. What I saw made me laugh so hard I thought I'd drop her down hard on the toilet seat again. There, floating on top of the toilet water was a perfectly-coiled brown rope of effluence. Ever seen a deliciously sweet Mexican churro frying in a large pot of hot oil? You get the idea.

"That, my precious one, is the most perfect turd I've ever seen in my life. It looks just like the coiled pattern on the rock you chose, the one you're still holding in your hand."

"Really?" she asked, contemplating the design on the flat rock. "What do you think that means?"

"I really don't know," I answered as I helped her pull her pants back up.

"Maybe it's reminding me to be thankful," she suggested, holding the smooth rock up so we could both see it. "I know that I'm eternally grateful to you."

Millions of family caregivers have to deal with the bodily wastes of their loved ones, and this experience made me realize how much love and trust Bee had to have in order to ask for this kind of assurance. And what's better is that she was completely okay with it.

We are both okay. We are more than okay. In Bee's words we are both *thrivers,* not merely survivors.

When we parted later that day she turned to me and said, as if she was uttering these words for the first time: "I am living in the light of God. I am a happy child of God. I am. I am. I am. I am a success, and I am worth it."

13. A Gamble in Reno

"It takes extreme bravery
to let someone see you when you're shitty."
– Bee Landis

Everyone at the care center had heard about Bee's upcoming trip to Reno. She'd been excited as a magpie for days, squawking about it with anyone who came within earshot of her room. She had a doctor's appointment there to check out an unusual lesion on her forehead that was becoming alarmingly inflamed and, proud as a puppy, she told me she was already up, washed, and dressed when I called to make sure she would be ready when I arrived to pick her up.

Her choice of clothing for this trip would have made a circus clown envious. She was wearing a Hawaiian shirt – all greens, oranges, blacks and browns – covering a pair of bubblegum-pink pants. On her feet were purple and red striped socks and no shoes. Grumbling about her coat being stolen (again), I grabbed a red, white, and blue light-weight jacket to add to the rainbow palette she had chosen for our four-hour drive to Reno. I suggested she might want to wear some shoes, too.

"I'm so excited," she repeated over and over again, while allowing me to put her shoes on her feet. "If I wasn't so out of it I'd have the good sense to be scared. Do you think we'll have bad weather? Everyone told me the weather was going to be stormy. I was hoping you wouldn't walk in here this morning and cancel the trip."

"Not to worry, Bee," I assured her. "I checked the weather before I left, and aside from a few raindrops here and there, we'll be just fine."

She settled comfortably into the passenger seat, gazing out the window at the high desert landscape. Bee had shrunk a bit, perhaps as much from her stooped posture as from gravity. If you were standing outside my truck looking at her through the passenger-side window, all you'd see would be her spiky, white hair, a blotchy forehead and two blue eyeballs staring back at you, reminding me of one of those ubiquitous *Kilroy Was Here* wall doodles during World War II.

Fall in the Sierra makes for one of the most exquisite drives imaginable. Aspen trees and towering cottonwoods, aglow in their golden autumnal splendor accompanied us almost the entire way. One tree after another gave Bee an opportunity to point while uttering grateful *ooohs* and *ahhhs*. The look on her face was that of an irreproachable child seeing only the beauty that life has to offer. Even highway signs caught her attention as she'd speak each one out loud slowly, as if she was just learning to read.

"Re-No...wun-hundred...mi-uls...LeeVi...ning...Mo...No...Lake."

At least 99% of her excitement about this trip had to do with a planned meeting with her son Larry, who'd agreed to join us for lunch after her dermatologist appointment. But Larry called at the last minute to say he "just couldn't break free," adding that he could meet us at the doctor's office after her appointment, "but only for a few minutes." If I wanted to see someone age before my eyes, this would have been the time. However, Bee was quick and effective at covering up her disappointment with an acquiescent "oh well" and my only prayer was that Larry would keep his word... this time.

The other meager 1% involved Bee's seeing one of her favorite people, her dermatologist, whom she simply called Tony. Tony had been Bee's doctor for several years, during which time he had removed various pathologies that cropped up periodically on her face. He was a good guy, Bee always said, quick to smile and "not so serious all the time," a distinction that ranked high on Bee's list of virtues.

As charming as a Southern minister after church on Sunday, Tony threw his arms around Bee instantly when he saw her, exclaiming how he missed her bright red hair. He even allowed me to accompany him into the operating room so I could observe his deft handiwork on Bee.

After Tony performed the ED&C (electrodessication & curettage), he took a biopsy of another dark, black mark above her right eye.

"Just in case," he said. "If it's a melanoma," he added, "it could kill her."

Taking him aside, I queried about the necessity for yet another surgical procedure on a woman Bee's age. To his credit, he thought about it for a couple of minutes, finally agreeing, "I see what you're saying. There wouldn't be any real need to do that. Let's see what happens with the pathology report."

The biopsy came back benign two weeks later.

After the surgery, Bee and I sat in the reception area waiting for Larry to arrive. She stared over my shoulder for thirty minutes, watching everyone who walked through the door. "Maybe this is him," she'd say, and then, completely dejected when she saw that it was not, she would cast her eyes down for a moment, only to check back at the door again and again.

Finally, Larry walked in and her face lit up like a Roman candle. Full of apologies, he embraced his mother, who instantly forgot about everything save his presence. But anger exploded inside of me with the weight of ten sticks of dynamite. Forget everything I'd ever learned about compassionate understanding. Right then, right there in Tony's waiting room, all I wanted to do was knock Larry into the next county. Instead, I encouraged him to be alone with his mother, excusing myself while I went outside and screamed in the parking lot for 15 minutes.

A wise teacher once helped me manage my need to control other people, situations and circumstances that were clearly *beyond* my control. "Your need to understand is your need to control," the wise teacher offered kindly, patient with my *yeah-but* objections. But as I stormed around amongst the cars in the parking lot, those wise words completely escaped me, replaced by *How could he? Doesn't he understand how important he is to her? What in the hell is the matter with him anyway? Why would he want to hurt her so much?*

I've rarely thought of myself as a caregiver. Instead, I prefer to see myself as a friend and advocate, one who gives a shit about another human being, one who will watch another's back and basically take on anyone who appears like they may cause harm, including Bee's son. Every time I would casually blurt out, "I'm a little angry at your son, Bee," she would remind me that he was doing the best he could with what he knew. No other love is as loyal as that of a mother to her children. And more to the point, she was telling the truth. Most of us *are* doing the best we can with what we know.

Finally I composed myself enough to re-enter the building where Larry was saying goodbye to Bee. I suddenly remembered a version of

125

Malachy McCourt's quote that says: "Resentment is like taking poison and waiting for the *other* person to die." Thankful that Larry showed up at all, I realized holding on to resentment would not serve either of us.

Mumbling something about needing to get back to work, Larry turned to me and offered a round of gratitude that completely caught me off guard.

"Thank you so much for all you do for my mom," he said. "You have no idea how comforting it is for me to know you are in her life. With my work and the kids and all, it's really hard to get down to Bishop. Well, just thanks, that's all. I'll try and call her more. I promise."

And, with that, he was out the door. Bee and I stood silently, watching him scurry back to his car.

Before embarking on the ten-hour round trip to Reno, I had some concerns that the trip might be too stressful for her. She hadn't had much stimulation in the last two years, and I didn't have a clue how she would respond. As it turned out, Bee was a real trooper. Periodically I would catch her napping for a few minutes, her head sloped down to where her chin and chest became one.

I have learned so much from this bewildering woman, who alternated between being a pure expression of Spirit, and a simple human lost in a web of denied emotions. Maybe we're all a little like that, seeking the Truth of who we are while constantly succumbing to false beliefs of incompetence and unworthiness.

Wanting to give Bee room to either share about her visit with Larry or not, I offered up some small talk on our way back to Bishop.

"I've been listening to a stimulating CD by Alan Wolf on Quantum Physics," I said nonchalantly. "Do you have any interest in hearing it?"

"I feel sorry for my son," she said, ignoring my question. "I know he feels rotten. He came up with more than he'd ever allowed come out of his mouth today."

This was the first time she had said a word about the content of their conversation. I was all ears, encouraging her to tell me more.

"I want to get into thinking about living and forgiving. I have to open up my hand and let him discover his own life."

"What a grand idea, Bee." I said. "When we keep seeing someone in a negative way, they have a tendency to stay that way, so why don't we *both* let him out of the box?"

When we reached the top of the grade the sun had already set behind the mountains, casting a giant shadow across the Owens Valley. Bee had been silent for a long while, happy to gaze out the window at the pinion pines and desert rock formations. She picked up the CD I had talked about earlier.

"I'd like to listen to this now," she said.

Knowing how the abstractions of quantum physics can make *my* brain sizzle, I hesitated a minute.

"This is pretty rough on the brain, Bee," I said.

"Oh that's okay," she replied. "My brain needs to exercise some."

As we listened to a couple of minutes on atoms, molecules and sub-atomic particles, I noticed that Bee had fallen asleep again, her head plopped back down on her chest (quantum physics can do that to a person). But two minutes later she sat straight up again, saying something about needing to take a nap when she got back. Was she unaware that she had just been asleep?

"Good idea," I said, just as we arrived at the care center. Her walker leading the way, Bee passed quickly through the halls toward her room while I talked with the nursing director about future hospice care in the facility. When I came to Bee's room a few minutes later to say goodbye, she was already sound asleep, snoring peacefully.

The curtain that separated Bee's bed from her roommate's was closed, so when I heard her roommate struggling to get out of bed, I walked around the curtain to see if I could be of assistance.

"Help me," she pleaded, while vainly attempting to climb over the bedrails.

As I stepped forward to help I was startled by the sound of a shrill alarm screeching in the vicinity of Bee's bed. I leapt around the curtain to find Bee in a full-fledged grand mal seizure, her body stiff as concrete, convulsing wildly. Her eyes were rolled back in her head, and through clenched teeth she was hissing like a snake through rivers of saliva that foamed around her mouth. It was terrifying to witness, but I managed to push the emergency button connected to her bed, and within seconds one of the aides came rushing into the room, followed by Bob, her nurse, who started barking orders.

"Get her head up," he yelled. "Turn her head to the side."

Swiftly, Bob had taken all of the appropriate measures to insure Bee's safety, including placing her on oxygen and giving her medication to relax her body. A feeling of utter uselessness overcame me, and all I could do was stroke her shoulder and say, "Its okay, Bee. I'm here. I love you. It's okay."

Thankfully, the seizure lasted only a few minutes, and then she went limp, and I knew from her past seizures that she would be out of it for the rest of the night. These seizures involve electric discharges in the brain, and one lasting longer than five minutes could result in sustained brain damage due to lack of oxygen. This one, thankfully, did not last longer than a minute or two. Part of me speculated about whether her odd on-again-off-again sleepiness on the drive home and urgent need to get into her bed was an unconscious awareness of the impending seizure.

It had been an intense day, and the drive back up the hill gave me some time to think about Bee, the violent seizure I'd witnessed, and all that had happened with Larry. I knew Bee was safe, with a loving, caring support staff that would check on her around the clock and call me if anything changed. Larry's final words echoed around in the recesses of my mind. Had I heard him correctly? He promised he'd try to call her more. Bee was right next to me when he said it, but didn't say a word, not even "yeah right. I've heard that before." She *believed* him, and that's what mothers do. I remembered a particularly prophetic conversation we had in August of 2005, where she acknowledged that she "maybe wasn't such a good mother when Larry was young."

> BEE: I think about Larry a lot now. There are things I think I feel guilty about, maybe attitudes I had. When I try to let him know that, he doesn't want to hear it.
>
> KELSEY: How do you know that?
>
> B: Because he feels guilty, too.
>
> K: How do you know *that?*

B: Because I can feel it.

K: But maybe these are more your feelings than Larry's.

B: The problem is I don't remember, and he does. I just *feel* the guilt and don't know why. I realize for the first time in my life that the things I have been criticizing in people have opened the door of understanding for me so I can see myself in those "sins."

K: I understand what you mean completely. That which I judge negatively in another is probably within me, too.

B: Larry obviously didn't like what he got as a kid. Sometimes you have to make something hurt in order to have it right. I'm having a hard time with my words... when you were a kid, did you ever have to shake something, like your finger, in order to get it to stop hurting?

K: I think I understand that.

B: That's what I'm doing. I'm always trying to make something stop.

K: What would happen if rather than trying to make it stop, you climbed on board to see where the pain was taking you?

B: I'm beginning to make sense out of this whole thing.

K: It's all connected, isn't it?

B: There's no ignoring it.

K: So, if we stopped resisting and started accepting, what would we have?

B: Maybe there's a miracle due us.

There certainly was a miracle due. It just took longer than my impatience could gracefully accept. After the trip to Reno, Bee's surgery, the frustrations with Larry, his subsequent offer of gratitude, and Bee's seizure, things started to shift a little. Larry called Bee the next day and again the next day and the next and the next. She became accustomed to his now daily attention, and during our morning chats she floated on loving clouds of joy, breathlessly sharing the latest news with me... "Oh you will be so thrilled when I tell you what Larry told me this morning!"

14. Something Purple

"If I can't laugh my way into heaven, I won't go."
– Bee Landis

"I hope God doesn't say, 'Well, Bee, it's time to go,'
because my room isn't straight enough yet."
– Bee Landis

The call came a little before midnight. I've learned to dread those middle-of-the-night phone calls for good reason. They initiate racing heartbeats, pit-of-the-stomach heaviness and a paralyzing hesitation to pick up the phone. Rarely does one hear good news delivered when awakened out of a sound sleep in the middle of the night.

"Hello, Kelsey, this is Brianne from the care center," the young female voice announced. "Bee had a serious seizure about a half an hour ago and now she isn't responding at all. Her blood pressure is dropping dangerously and her heartbeat is over 180 bpm."

Seven months earlier I'd received a similar phone call from the same nurse. That time, fortunately, I was only 45 minutes away.

The eerie sequence of events began with a violent grand mal seizure followed by a precipitous drop in blood pressure and no response. That time I flew out of bed and was in my car within five minutes heading down the grade to the care center. Remembering that the California Highway Patrol was generally off the roads between midnight and 5:00 am in that rural area, I maintained close to triple-digit speeds most of the way down to Bishop.

Although Bee had been having sporadic seizures every two to four weeks, she would always respond to physical sensations immediately following the brain attacks, and would recover completely within 24 hours. But this time the urgency in Brianne's voice indicated that I needed to get down there as quickly as possible.

Several nurses, including Brianne, were checking Bee's vitals when I stepped into the room. Their faces were compassionately passive,

133

as if the bell had already tolled in their minds and it was only a matter of time. Respectfully they left me alone with Bee when I walked closer to where she lay, unmoving, her mouth open slightly. I remember her still face, harshly illuminated by the strip of fluorescent lights above her bed, and reached up to pull the white cord that turned the damned things off.

There was no response from Bee when I called her name, quite loudly actually, as I leaned down within inches of her left ear. No eye movement or twitches to indicate that she recognized my voice. There was no response when I picked up the thin left hand that lay heavily across her chest and squeezed it tightly. Was it all coming to this moment, I wondered? No fanfare, no sirens, nothing that prepared me for the moment when I would watch Bee take her final breath. It was all strangely surreal, and yet I felt prepared for anything, because I trusted Bee's intent to manifest her exit strategy as we had discussed almost a year earlier. There was one problem: I was there with her and in her exit strategy, she said I wouldn't be.

"How long did you say she's she been like this?" I asked Brianne when she returned a few minutes later.

"About two hours," she answered softly, as if not wanting to wake Bee. That felt odd to me, speaking in hushed tones around the dying, as if our loud voices might encourage the dying one back to earth.

I sat next to Bee for more than an hour, softly stroking her arms, her face and her short white, butch-cut hair. Large brownish-red spots littered her forehead and cheeks, signs of small skin cancers that accumulated through the lifetime of an 86 year-old woman who spent too much time in the sun as a young girl. Every once in a while I would take a tissue and wipe the saliva pooling at the sides of her mouth. Nothing penetrated the netherworld in which she was drifting. A raspy, guttural sound emanated from her throat as she breathed in and out. Although Brianne hadn't used the word *comatose*, Bee's breathing sounded identical to the breathing sounds my mother made when she was in a deep coma a few days before her death.

It occurred to me that it might be time to call Larry, but Bee's blood pressure, although considerably low, had stabilized for the moment, and I felt no need to awaken him and his family in the middle of the night until absolutely necessary.

Another hour went by with practically no change in Bee's condition. It was extremely important to Bee that neither she nor anyone around her suffer when she made her transition. Was she suffering now? What does suffering look like in another? Is it as subjective as what makes someone angry or happy?

None of these questions was immediately answered, however a previous conversation between Larry and me raced into my mind. When Bee chose to take herself off of the anti-seizure medication a couple of years earlier, I'd called Larry to let him know about her decision. He told me his greatest fear was that Bee would suffer an incapacitating stroke as a result of continued seizures. Remembering that conversation caused me to think the unthinkable.

It pains me to admit it here, but I know in my deepest heart that many caregivers have contemplated the same thing. What if Bee recovered only to find herself unable to do what matters to her most... communicate? Would she want me to help her to eliminate that possibility? Could I place the pillow that was lying only a few inches away from me over her face long enough to stop her breathing, releasing her to the beautiful heaven of which she so often spoke? Would she know? Would it help? Would I get caught in the act of helping my sweet friend make an easier transition? This was *not* something we'd discussed in our conversations about her exit strategy.

Over and over I asked these questions, sometimes silently to myself and sometimes out loud to Bee, as if willing her to make it clear to me what she wanted. I watched my hand stroke the pillow, squeezing it, sensing if it was thick enough to do the job correctly, swiftly, without causing her to suffer any more. Surely I had witnessed this scene in movies a dozen times. But most of those fictional depictions were carried out as either murder – *Sopranos* style – or altruistically, as when the Chief Bromden character suffocated the lobotomized R.P. McMurphy in *One Flew over the Cuckoos Nest*. A friend of mine once shared that he helped his terminally ill father in the exact same way. It was a supreme act of kindness and compassion, and he knew without question that it was the right and moral thing to do. Recalling his heartfelt story did not make my decision any easier.

A few moments later Bee made the decision for me when she opened her eyes, as if waking from a long, restful nap, and said, "Oh, you're here. I'm so glad. Is it morning yet?" And then she promptly lost consciousness again.

I was stupefied, but that five-second communication was all I needed to tell me what to do, or in this case, what not to do.

At dawn I called Larry, alerting him to Bee's condition and the possibility of it worsening, and suggested that he make the four-hour drive to be with his mother. Sometimes miracles arrive via the most mystifying delivery systems. To this day I'm convinced that Bee just wanted to have her son and grandsons come down and visit with her for a while. It had been more than a year since she had seen them.

Now it was seven months later, and this time I was in my home in Oregon when the phone call came. When I asked Brianne if she thought this was different than Bee's most recent "dry run," she said yes, adding that she wanted to put Bee on oxygen. Without hesitation, I said, "No. Please don't. I'll call you back in a few minutes."

Taking a deep breath, I leaned over and turned on the bedside lamp, feeling my eyes burn from the sudden brightness. Yoda, my one-eyed cat, was curled into a soft, calico ball at the foot of my bed and meowed grumpily when I threw back the blankets, unintentionally hurling her to the floor. After a quick stop in the bathroom and a quick wash of my face to clear the sleep away, I headed for the meditation chair in the corner of my room to "connect" with Bee.

Within two or three minutes I heard a familiar song from the 1970s, one that I hadn't heard for at least two decades. It was by the group Rare Earth:

I just want to celebrate, yeah, yeah
I just want to celebrate, yeah, yeah
Another day of living,
I just want to celebrate another day of life.[17]

---

[17] Rare Earth in Concert, Fekaris/Zesses 1971

Clearly, this was not a "normal" meditation experience for me; I had to resolve what this song meant, especially since it wouldn't exactly have been on the top ten lists of songs Bee would remember either.

"Bee?" I asked as if she were sitting on my lap. "Does this mean that you want another day, that you want to live longer?"

Her answer, in the clearest, most enthusiastic voice I'd heard from her in years, was "No... substitute the word 'way' for 'day.'"

I just want to celebrate
another WAY of living.

It was then that I knew that she had already left her body and was simply delighting in her new *way* of living, her newfound freedom without the strains and pains of an 87 year-old body.

Ten minutes later Brianne called back to tell me Bee was gone.

By 1:00 in the morning when I rolled out of my long driveway, I had called my closest friend, Janet, to tell her the news, asking for her help with feeding my dogs, cats and horses. The second call was to my household caretaker of many years, praying that she was available to continue caring for the critters until I returned. Eternally grateful for my friends, I left the house, confident that all was well. The unfaltering kindness of friends shines like a rainbow when we are in the midst of weathering our personal storms.

The third call was to Larry in Reno. Responding as if he had expected the call, we agreed to meet at the care center at noon to talk about Bee's wishes, make arrangements for her cremation, and plan a tribute for the coming weekend.

The Oregon Outback Scenic Byway, a 171-mile, two-lane country road that connects Hwy. 97 just south of La Pine to Hwy. 395 in Lakeview, is normally a feast for the eyes, with vast, open rangeland and giant red citadels. But all I saw on this middle-of-the-night excursion was what was illuminated within 500 feet of my truck's headlights. Everywhere else I looked was pitch-black. To make matters worse, I'd never been one who stays up late, and my night vision isn't good, so I normally avoid driving after dark. The urge to sleep kept nagging at my body, necessitating my using every trick in the book to stay awake.

137

Sticking my head out the window worked splendidly for a while, especially since the outside temperature was hovering in the low teens.

Once the hair inside my nostrils began to freeze, I closed the window, cranked up the music, and started tugging on my earlobes, another strategy I learned when I took driver's education in high school. These gimmicks worked sufficiently to get me to Alturas, a close-knit community south of the Oregon border, where I could fill up with gas.

During the three-and-a-half hours it took me to get to Alturas, I gave full reign to whatever emotions needed a voice, giving them their time in the spotlight. Strangely, deep, penetrating mournfulness wasn't one of them. Not that there weren't tears of sadness with the realization that my life as I had known it for ten years was about to change drastically. Stabbing, incapaciting pains of loss I hadn't felt since the death of my son. But a greater reality, a greater Truth had a louder voice, validating that Bee perfectly executed her exit strategy, down to the most minute details. That awareness trumped all other feelings of loss and pain in favor of a desire to shout to the heavens, "Yahoo for you, Bee!"

It was fun to hear Bee's familiar voice come through periodically, insisting that everything was alright. "You're in good company," she said. "Just you and God."

"Alfalfa" met me at the door of the care center when I arrived at around 11:30 a.m. The name was an affectionate moniker I'd given to the physical therapist four years earlier, when Bee first moved into Room 117 at the nursing facility. Nothing was said between us, just a knowing, tender embrace from a very kind man that gave me permission to release a few more buckets of tears.

Alfalfa followed me down to Bee's room. All of the photographs of Bee's family and her meager collection of clothing were already boxed up and put away in a storage room down the hall. How quickly and impersonally life moves on.

There was little to do in terms of paperwork, as all of that had been put into place seven months earlier. When Larry arrived we hugged each other, cried a bit together, and acknowledged our delight that Bee had made her transition on her terms. Larry agreed to contact the local newspaper in Bishop to have Bee's obituary placed in the Saturday edition so that her old friends and members of her church could be notified of her passing and the tribute we were planning for the next day.

Not that this is altogether uncommon, but frequently there is a "rallying" of sorts just before someone dies, like a ninth-inning explosion of runs by the losing team in baseball. There's no real absolute here, just something I've observed in my hospice work for many years, and certainly Bee was no exception.

For ten days Bee's memory, clarity of mind and ability to express herself had been unprecedented. Four days before her death she asked a staff member to bring her a phone book because she wanted to look up an old friend, someone with whom she'd started her Science of Mind church. Not only did Bee remember the woman's name perfectly, she also recalled much of what they'd done together nearly three decades earlier. This is extremely unusual for a person with moderate dementia, who in recent months would forget who she was talking to when *I* was on the phone with her. Her friend was astounded to know that Bee was alive and living in the care center, and joyfully agreed to come over and bring her a hamburger and French fries, Bee's favorite lunch. When I called the friend to tell her of Bee's death, she was as shocked as one could imagine, regaling me with how lucid Bee had been when they were together only a few days earlier.

Although Larry wanted to write Bee's obituary, I asked if it would be alright to include this line: *If you are planning to attend the Celebration of Life for Bee tomorrow, please wear something purple.*

It was Bee's favorite color, and every single one of her friends knew it. There was only one problem. In my haste to get down to Bishop I didn't pay any attention to what clothing I packed, and didn't give a thought to what I'd wear to her memorial services. Not one item of clothing in my suitcase had anything purple in it.

There are few apparel stores in the little town of Bishop, which is home to only 17,000 residents. *K-Mart* is the largest supplier of clothing, but that just wouldn't do. So I did what I knew to do best... ask The Source. It was Bee's familiar voice that came through, loud and clear.

"You know that store on the corner of West Line Street and Main? The one with all the wedding dresses in the window. Go there and ask Jeanette. She'll help you."

At least a hundred times over the years Bee and I passed the corner where this store sat, but never had I browsed there, and as far as I know, neither had Bee.

Wedding garments of all shapes and sizes lined the walls of the store, but the first thing I saw when I opened the door, way up high behind a rack of bridesmaid dresses, was a bright purple, feathered hat.

A few customers were rummaging around the racks as I snuck around the corner to get a closer look. I put the hat on and stared in disbelief at myself in the mirror. "There is no way I am going to wear this hat, Bee. It reminds me of Cruella De Ville in *101 Dalmatians*. No way."

Bee's answer was patiently kind as she reminded me, "Go ask Jeanette and she'll help you."

By this time there was only one other person in the store, an older woman sitting behind the glass display case in the corner of the room, smiling at me.

"Excuse me. Are you Jeanette?" I asked, without much conviction.

"Yes, I am," she answered. "How can I help you?"

"Do you know Bee Landis?"

"Well, yes I do. For over thirty years."

"Oh, my. Bee passed away a few days ago, and I'm doing her tribute tomorrow at her church. I asked people to wear something purple and I realized I didn't bring anything with me and please don't think I'm crazy, but Bee said you would help me."

It was one of those moments where I could completely understand why anyone would reach for the phone to call for the mental health squad. But Jeanette casually reached up behind her to a hook on her right and pulled down a grape Kool-Aid-colored scarf, long and luxurious, complete with silver sparkles.

"Will this do?"

"Perfectly," I answered as I wrapped the scarf around my neck.

"And," she added, reaching for a pair of light-amethyst-colored earrings that sat right in the middle of the display case in front of her, "These might work, too."

Don't let anyone tell you that we can't communicate with our loved ones after they die. Souls don't go anywhere after death. Instead, they actually go *everywhere* all at once, and all we humans left behind need to do is open our hearts to allow these cherished souls to reveal their existence to us. This extraordinary experience with Bee's precise direction filled me with such love and comfort that I felt like I could simply fly out of the store if I wanted to.

Although I was going to perform the service at the Celebration of Life for Bee, it was Larry's job to fill in the blanks during the 64 years of Bee's life before I met her. To say that I was fearful of what he might say would be too dramatic, but I did feel some concern. An almost life-sized photograph of a younger, red-headed Bee dressed in a long, ceremonial dark blue robe was positioned right next to Larry when he stood in front of the packed church. Even in a one-dimensional form it appeared that Bee was looking at everyone individually in the room, no matter where they sat.

At that moment, right before my welcoming eyes, every little doubt I had ever had about Larry vanished like dust particles in the wind. For ten minutes he spoke from an authentically loving son's heart about his now-departed mother, becoming wiser, kinder and more virtuous with every funny, shared memory of her journey. It didn't so much matter what words he chose or how humorously he recalled Bee's charming antics. It was the honey in his voice that got me, the sweetest sound a mother could ever want to hear, brimming with love and respect, and most of all, with gratitude that she was his mother. Did I imagine it or was that really Bee leaping up and down in the back of the room with flashy, metallic pom-poms (purple, of course) in her hands and a tooth-filled grin that stretched all the way across the Sierra?

After Larry's speech, I stood before the standing-room-only gathering of friends, former congregation members, Larry, his wife, and Bee's two grandsons, Michael and Andy. As I slowly scanned the room, blinking away tears of joy, I noticed that every single person, all the women *and* all the men, were wearing something purple.

EPILOGUE

While wondering what to write for this epilogue, I took a break from my computer to perform my annual spring weeding ritual. Blasting out of my outdoor speakers was Harry Connick, Jr.'s rendition of "If I Only Had a Brain" from *The Wizard of Oz* and it got me to thinkin', as Bee used to say.

Dark clouds filled the sky; having just deposited a rainstorm that made the water on my pond look like it was boiling. The soggy soil made weed picking a snap.

One of my dogs was watching me intently with a "voice" so loud that I couldn't ignore him.

"Would you please throw the damn ball already," he seemed to say, but then he would settle back on his haunches until I stopped what I was doing long enough to pick up the damn ball and throw it already.

Patience is like that — at least for a dog. And perhaps patience is one of the virtues that dogs are here to teach us, along with unconditional love, of course. Learning patience may be one of the hardest lessons on earth for most of us, but through diligent practice and years of seeing that an impatient person is not generally a happy person, we may eventually be able to claim that virtue.

My relationship with Bee functioned as a luminous flashlight on the "patience factor" in me, raising it to a higher level than I could have managed without her. For that I will be eternally grateful, as will my friends who've been pleading with me for years to be more patient. There were days when I wanted to hang up on Bee when she was being particularly sarcastic on the phone, which was her form of emotional camouflage for the anger (translation: fear) she was feeling, but didn't quite know how to express. Dementia can do that to a person. A forgotten promise or a thwarted expectation, coupled with little or no memory of what the promise or expectation was, can lead to a very frustrated elder.

"What can I do to make your world more wonderful?" I'd ask Bee often during our morning talks.

"You could come see me," she'd answer, knowing that I would find a way to do it. And, for ten years, I made that drive at least every eight weeks.

But most of the time elders *won't* ask. They're proud people, many of them weaned on hardship and self-sufficiency, so asking for help or support isn't easy. Often the request gets translated into whining or complaining, especially if there has been a lot of drama or abuse in their family histories. But when someone comes in from outside the family unit and befriends an elder just because they want to and not because they feel obliged, the asking is a thousand times easier.

Our elders are simply asking for a few minutes of our time and for our complete and uncompromising *emotional* presence. It's a presence that listens with genuine interest in what they have to say. It's a presence that asks questions about their lives, their contributions, and what matters to them. And it works both ways, because both the elder and the caregiver are fulfilled in that process.

During the talks I give on the subject of adopting elders, I'm often asked how one would begin the process of finding an elder to adopt. The answer is as simple as walking into your local nursing facility and asking the administrator which patients aren't visited by family or friends. Once you get inside a facility it won't be difficult to find one to adopt. Without exception, every administrator I've talked to said they would be happy to match up outside visitors with lonely patients. Ultimately, they realize, a happier, more satisfied patient is a good thing for everyone, including the staff.

But the match has to be a good fit. As an example, another elder I adopted, "Eleanor," was 94 when I met her, and had been living in an elder foster care home for three months. A close friend and business associate of hers shared pieces of her personal story, using phrases such as "very difficult," "angry with the world" and "not someone who would be amenable to a visit from anyone in the outside world." Thankfully, (and with the friend's blessings) I didn't listen to that gloomy forecast, but decided to find out on my own who Eleanor was.

What I found was a bright, resilient, and deeply grateful woman who shared her dreams of someday building a house and starting another business. When I brought up the subject of her exit strategy, she didn't hesitate.

"It will be sooner than I think," she said, matter-of-factly. "And I am just fine with that. I'm quite ready."

Eleanor and I were a good fit.

It seems that everyone these days is absolutely crazy about making their "TO DO" lists. Feel free to think of one on your own, but just in case, here's one that may get you started:

1. Open your heart.

2. If you don't know of a nursing facility near you, do an on-line search or open your yellow pages and find one.

3. Call the facility and ask if you may come in and "adopt an elder" who isn't visited regularly by anyone.

4. Show up.

5. Open your heart.

6. When you get to meet the elder that is a good fit, share with them why you are there, who you are, and then...

7. Open your heart.

8. Listen to what the elder has to give to you. Empty yourself of any ideas of a preconceived outcome.

9. Keep coming back. Be consistent and keep your word.

10. Open your heart to receive more miracles than you ever dreamed possible in this exchange.

Long ago I studied the philosophy of Confucius, and there was one quote I remember distinctly. It said, "No matter how busy you may think you are, you must find time for reading, or surrender yourself to self-chosen ignorance."

I know Confucius would forgive me if I switched a few words around, because it beautifully relates to another gift I received from Bee:

No matter how busy you may think you are, you must find time to sit with the elders, or surrender yourself to self-chosen ignorance of what they have learned and what they have to teach you.

I was thoroughly humbled when Bee shared with me one day, "When we can truly accept an unlimited God Source, only then can we accept an unlimited self." The day she said that we were sitting in my truck overlooking the deep, blue expanse of Lake Sabrina, about 30 miles west of Bishop. I asked her what she meant by an "unlimited self."

"It's like this lake here," she answered, pointing to the wind ripples shimmering across the water's surface. "It's been here for millions of years and yet you and I can only see the top of it. We can only see the reflection of the sky or the mountains on it. There's so much more down there we *can't* see from here. There's life there that we can only imagine. We're like that. There's so much more to us than we know."

At this point I can only imagine a life without hearing Bee's child-like giggles in the morning, or how fun it was to share the *Daily Word* with her everyday, or how much fun it was to paint her toenails and wash her hair, and listen, at her feet, as she fed my soul with her evocative Beeisms.

Reflecting back over the weeks preceding Bee's death, I noticed Bee's hunger for fulfillment and completion of the personal goals she had set prior to her death. For years Bee shared with me how deeply the tentacles of guilt and unworthiness had permeated her very being. In the weeks before she died, she realized and released all of "those contaminating thoughts" that perverted how she saw herself in the world. She wanted to express gratitude for *everything* — every single flower she saw bloom outside her window in the spring, every small kindness she received from someone.

Interestingly, the care center's administrator, Jerry Vaculin, just happened to be walking down the hall at 7:00pm the night Bee passed away, providing the perfect opportunity for her to fulfill her goal of complete grace and gratitude, specifically to him, who not only cared deeply for her welfare for years, but he made her laugh and laugh. Bee's laughter was a gift that kept on giving to everyone around her. I can still hear her chuckling... even now.

"Hey, BM!" she yelled from her bed, using the ribald initials for Boss Man, as she jokingly referred to him. "C'mere, I want to tell you something."

Jerry told me he saw a healthy, vibrant Bee, sitting up in her bed, pillows all fluffed up behind her head. "She just told me she was really grateful for all I had done for her. She told me I was doing a good job. It made my day."

Throughout this wondrous internal spelunking experience, my own awareness has increased exponentially because of Bee. My death is no longer an unknown, unexplored cavern inside of me, but an eventuality that I embrace fully. I do want my stay here on earth to come to a quick conclusion, whenever it happens. The actual cause is not as important as having sufficient time to see it coming so that I can consciously say, "Oh here you are. I'm ready. I have no regrets. What a precious life it has been."

And no one, including me, will suffer.

Thanks for the nudge, Bee.

~~~~~~~~~~~~~~~~~~~~~~~~~

RULE NUMBER SIX

Two prime ministers are sitting in a room discussing affairs of state. Suddenly a man bursts in, apoplectic with fury, shouting and stamping and banging his fist on the desk.

The resident prime minister admonishes him, "Peter," he says, "kindly remember Rule Number 6," whereupon Peter is instantly restored to complete calm, apologizes, and withdraws.

The politicians return to their conversation, only to be interrupted yet again twenty minutes later by a hysterical woman gesticulating wildly, her hair flying. Again the intruder is greeted with the words: "Marie, please remember Rule Number 6."

Complete calm descends once more, and she too withdraws with a bow and an apology. When the scene is repeated for a third time, the visiting prime minister addresses his colleague, "My dear friend, I've seen many things in my life, but never anything as remarkable as this. Would you be willing to share with me the secret of Rule Number 6?"

"Very simple," replies the resident prime minister. "Rule Number 6 is 'Don't take yourself so damn seriously."

"Ah," says his visitor, "that is a fine rule."

After a moment of pondering, he inquires, "And what, may I ask, are the other rules?"

"There aren't any."

Reprinted with permission from the publisher, Hay House, Inc.
Copyright © 2004 by Wayne W. Dyer

RESOURCES

AGING WITH DIGNITY (FIVE WISHES PROGRAM)
PO Box 1661
Tallahassee, FL 32302-1661
(888) 594-7437
fivewishes@agingwithdignity.org
www.agingwithdignity.org

My Wish For:
The Person I Want to Make Care Decisions For Me When I Can't.
The Kind of Medical Treatment I Want or Don't Want.
How Comfortable I Want to Be.
How I Want People to Treat Me.
What I Want My Loved Ones to Know.

SENIOR OUTLOOK
www.senioroutlook.com

A PLACE FOR MOM
www.aplaceformom.com

GENERAL INFORMATION
www.google.com
www.theyellowpages.com

NATIVE ELDERS
www.anelder.org

AGING CARE
(866) 627-2467
www.agingcare.com

AGING PARENTS AND ELDER CARE
www.aging-parents-and-elder-care.com

ASSIST GUIDE INFORMATION SERVICES
www.agis.com

CARE FOR CAREGIVERS OF ALZEIMER'S PATIENTS
www.theribbon.com

FOR CAREGIVERS, BY CAREGIVERS
(800) 829-2734
www.caregiver.com

ELDER CARE NEWS
www.eldercarenews.com

NON-MEDICAL HOME CARE
(888) 777-7630
www.griswoldspecialcare.com

NURSING HOME COMPARE
www.medicare.gov/NHCompare/home.asp

Printed in the United States
214318BV00001B/7/P